مَوْلِدُ الحَمْدِ الأَكْبَر

حَقَايِقُ الرَسُوْلِ الأَعْظَم
وَأَنْوَارُ النَبِيِّ العَلِيِّ
مِنْ كَلَامِ البَحْرِ الخِضَمْ
الشَّيْخِ الأَكْبَرِ ابْنِ العَرَبِيِّ

Mawlid of The Greatest Praise ﷺ

Realities of the Most August Messenger and Lights of the Lofty Prophet Muhammad ﷺ From the Speech of the Endless Ocean, the Greatest Master Ibn al-ʿArabī

Compiled and Translated by

Dr. Ali Hussain

Foreword by

Prof. Rudolph Bilal Ware

First Edition August 2023

ISBN: 978-1-938058-75-2

Printed in the United States of America.

Library of Congress Cataloging-in-Publication Data

TBD

Published and Distributed by:
Institute for Spiritual and Cultural Advancement
17195 Silver Parkway, #401
Fenton, MI 48430 USA
Tel: (810) 593-1222
Fax:(810) 815-0518
Email: info@sufilive.com
Web: http://www.sufilive.com
Photo Credit: Malika Ayyubi

Table of Contents

Foreword i
Introduction v
Chapter One: The Saints' Love for the Prophet ﷺ 1
Chapter Two: Introduction 7
Chapter Three: Holy Qur'an 11
Chapter Four: Informing of His Lofty Rank ﷺ 15
Chapter Five: His Reality ﷺ as a Walking Qur'an 23
Chapter Six: His Household ﷺ and Their Lofty Station 37
Chapter Seven: The Lofty Station of His Law ﷺ 45
Chapter Eight: His Ascension ﷺ 51
Chapter Nine: The Birth of His Reality ﷺ 55
Chapter Ten: Standing in Sight of the Full Moon ﷺ 65
Chapter Eleven: Benedictions Upon the Beloved ﷺ 81

بِسۡمِ ٱللَّهِ ٱلرَّحۡمَٰنِ ٱلرَّحِيمِ

Foreword

God blessed the pen of Ibn al-ʿArabi with a rare, perhaps singular gift. In the annals of Islamic literary history, one would be hard pressed to find an author more capable of chronicling the way of the wayfarer than *ash-Shaykh al-Akbar*. His oeuvre is a journal of the journey through rapturous states and exalted stations along The Path. His prose is poetry, and his poetry is transcendent.

There is, however, another chamber beyond poetry and prose in the writings of spiritual masters. This inner sanctum is beyond their didactic teachings, beyond their divinely inspired prose or poetry. These can be understood, in essence, as efforts to trace with ink their footfalls as they sought the Door of Return, or missives brought back from the spiritual plane and expressed in the tongue of the physical world.

Ṣalawāt on the other hand, Divine blessings on the Prophet ﷺ, occupy another register. These words are different. They are more than a roadmap of Return, and more than a translation of ascension. They are a *portal into* the mystical experience rather than a *window onto* it.

The sole surviving text we have of the Moroccan Sufi Ibn Mashish, the *Ṣalāt al-Mashīshiyya* is not a representation of Divine Illumination, but rather a reflection of it. And the whole of the spiritual tradition established by his student, Abu-Hasan al-Shadhili, is permeated with this same radiance. For in the first lines of his prayer Ibn Mashish invokes a blessing upon the one 'in whom *irrupted* the secrets, and from whom *erupted* the lights."

Similarly, *Jawharat al-Kamāl*, the blessing that God cast into the heart of another great North African Sufi Master, Ahmad Tijani, depicts for us the heart of the Messenger ﷺ as a jewel. It is a flawless gem in which the light of all meanings and spiritual understandings are refracted, imbuing all creation.

This blessing also refers to the Prophetic light as 'the wellspring of the Real," and "the rainclouds that fill all the oceans." Later adherents of the tradition, like the West African spiritual giants al-Hajj Umar Tall, and Shaykh al-Islam Ibrahim Niass, would channel this flood to irrigate two of the largest Sufi movements of the 19th and 20th centuries.

By recentering us on the *ṣalawāt* of Ibn al-ʿArabi, Dr. Ali Hussain is making a singular contribution to the modern history of Sufism, Spirituality, and Metaphysics. These words of Ibn al-ʿArabi are beyond narration, instruction, or translation – this is invocation. This is not a mere discussion of the mystical experience – it is the essence of tasting, and it is sorely needed in this era.

God has blessed the Pen of Dr. Ali Hussain with a rare perhaps singular gift. In our time, I know of none who drinks more deeply from the wellspring of *ash-Shaykh al-Akbar* and can think of none better to translate and present this sacred gift to us. He has a deep analytical and experiential understanding of Sufi thought, and the linguistic sophistication in Arabic and English to both hear the ineffable subtleties in the original, and to render them with beauty and grace.

Dr. Rudolph (Bilal) Ware

August 23, 2023
6 Safar, 1445
Santa Barbara, California

بِسْمِ اللَّهِ الرَّحْمَٰنِ الرَّحِيمِ

Introduction

"You have to be a poet to understand Ibn al-ʿArabī"
Mawlana Shaykh Hisham Kabbani

"For every age, there is one to ennoble it,
and I am, for that age, this one"
Shaykh al-Akbar Muhyiddin Ibn al-ʿArabi

All praise is due to God who facilitates for His servants to love Him, only because He loved them first. The height of that love manifests in prophets and messengers, most auspiciously in their master and leader, our beloved Muhammad ﷺ, his family, companions and those who follow them in guidance until the end of time.

Thenceforth, those who inherit that love and light from *sayyidi-l-wujūd* (the master of existence) ﷺ, his family and companions, become known as *awliyāʾ* (saints/friends of God), the pegs and mountains who carry divine secrets and serve as trustees over His creation. He gazes through them at the universe, and they are *ʿuyūnu-r-Raḥmān* (The Eyes of the Most-Merciful).

From among them, still few are chosen as *aqṭāb* (poles), or even a *ghawth* (succor) for creation, that singular representative who answers directly to our master

Muhammad ﷺ and carries out his wishes for *ummatu-l-da'wah* (entire creation) and *ummatu-l-ijābah* (community of believing Muslims).

Across generations, since the beginning of Islam through the blessed birth of *sayyidu-l-wujūd* ﷺ, there have been many such unique singularities: Sidi 'Abdul Qadir al-Jilani, Imam Abu Hamid al-Ghazali and, the heart of this book, al-Shaykh al-Akbar Muhyiddin Ibn al-'Arabi.

I first compiled this *mawlid* (a genre of sacred poetry commemorating the birth of the Prophet Muhammad ﷺ) in 2019. Since then, I have been waiting for the right moment to arrive when I feel the call in my heart to seek its publication, with the grace of God, His Beloved ﷺ and saints.

As we await to welcome the blessed lunar month of Rabi' al-Awwal in the year 1445/2023 and the occasion of the Prophet's birth ﷺ, I am humbled and honored to finally present this work to you, titled:

Mawlid al-Ḥamd al-Akbar:
Ḥaqā'iq al-Rasūl al-A'ẓam wa Anwar al-Nabiyyi al-'Aliyyi min Kalām al-Baḥr al-Khiḍam al-Shaykh al-Akbar Ibn al-'Arabī

Mawlid of the Greatest Praise:
Realities of the Most August Messenger and Lights of the Lofty Prophet Muhammad ﷺ From the Speech of the Endless Ocean the Greatest Master Ibn al-ʿArabi

This book is a humble attempt that follows in the footsteps of a long list of blessed works in the *mawlid* genre and praise poetry of the Prophet Muhammad ﷺ, such as *Mawlid al-Daybaʿi*, the *Burdah* by Imam al-Busairi, *Mawlid al-Ḍiyāʾ al-Lāmiʿ* (The Shimmering Light) by Habib ʿUmar b. Hafiz and countless others.

And it explicitly pays homage to those blessed works by adopting their structure and organization. Consisting of eleven chapters, the first introduces the *mawlid* with short remarks by our guides Shaykh Hisham Kabbani and Habib ʿUmar b. Hafiz ؓ about love of the Prophet Muhammad ﷺ and its importance in the lives of Muslims, believers, humanity and all of creation.

The second chapter is an introductory *qaṣīda* (ode), the likeness of which is found in *mawlid al-Daybaʿi, The Shimmering Light* and other works. The words of this ode are a versification of Shaykh al-Akbar Ibn al-ʿArabi's well-known short formula of *ṣalawāt* (benedictions upon the

Prophet Muhammad ﷺ) known as *al-ṣalāt al-muṭalsama* (The Enigmatic Benediction).

Chapter three is an opening of grace from the Holy Qur'an, following in the example of the aforementioned works in this genre. Thenceforth, chapters four through eight consist of direct excerpts from Shaykh al-Akbar's two most important works: *al-Futūḥāt al-Makkiyya* (The Meccan Openings) and *Fuṣūṣ al-Ḥikam* (The Bezels of Wisdom).

These chapters reveal the lofty status of the Prophet ﷺ in the sight of saints like Shaykh al-Akbar, as pertaining to themes like the Prophet ﷺ as a 'Walking Qur'an', the Prophetic Household and the reality of his *mi'rāj* (ascension) ﷺ.

Whereas other works in the *mawlid* genre usually discuss the physical birth of the Prophet ﷺ, this book focuses instead on the blessed birth of his reality ﷺ, known among Sufi saints as *al-ḥaqīqa al-muḥammadiyya* (the Muhammadan Reality) or *al-nūr al-muḥammadī* (the Muhammadan Light), which he ﷺ describes in a *ḥadīth* as God's first creation. This is the focus of chapter nine, which uses excerpts from a third work by Ibn al-'Arabi: *al-Tanazzulāt al-Mawṣiliyya* (The Divine Inspirations of Mosul).

The tenth chapter is *maḥall al-qiyām* (the place of standing) where, as is commonly found in all *mawlid* works, readers stand out of reverence and sing a series of poems celebrating the birth of the Prophet ﷺ. All the odes in this section have been composed by this poor compiler and translator of this work, following in the footsteps of his guides: Shaykh al-Akbar Ibn al-ʿArabi, Habib ʿUmar b. Hafiz and Shaykh Hisham Kabbani ؓ.

The last chapter, usually a concluding supplication, is another well-known *ṣalawāt* (prophetic benediction) by Ibn al-ʿArabi known as *al-ṣalāt al-fayḍiyya* (The Overflowing Benediction), which was been previously published and included in our collection of Ibn al-ʿArabi's litanies.

I ask God Almighty that He bless this endeavor, lifting whatever is good in it to His Presence ﷻ and delivering it to the threshold of His Beloved Prophet Muhammad ﷺ, his family, companions and saints ؓ.

Ali Hussain

August 23, 2023
6 Safar, 1445
Fenton, Michigan

بِسْمِ ٱللَّهِ ٱلرَّحْمَٰنِ ٱلرَّحِيمِ

Bismillāhi-r-Raḥmāni-r-Raḥīm
In the Name of God, Most Beneficent Most Merciful

الفَصْلُ الأَوَّلُ: مَحَبَّةُ الأَوْلِيَاءُ لِلنَّبِي ﷺ

Al-Faṣlu-l-Awwal: Maḥabbatu-l-Awliyā'i li-n-Nabiyy ﷺ
Chapter One: The Saints' Love for the Prophet ﷺ

يَقُولُ سَيِّدِي القُطْبُ المُتَصَرِّفُ الشَّيْخُ مُحَمَّد هِشَام قَبَّانِي حَفِظَهُ الله:

Yaqūlu Sayyidi-l-Quṭbu-l-Mutaṣarrifu ash-Shaykh Muḥammad Hishām Kabbānī ḥafiḍahu Allāh
Our Master, the Governor of Poles, Shaykh Muhammad Hisham Kabbani, Allah preserve him, says:

اَبْتَدِأُ بِقَوْلِ الحَمْدُ لله رَبِّ العَالَمِينَ وَالصَّلَاةُ وَالسَّلَامُ عَلَى أَشْرَفِ المُرْسَلِينَ سَيِّدِنَا وَنَبِيِّنَا مُحَمَّدٍ وَعَلَى آلِهِ وَصَحْبِهِ أَجْمَعِينَ الَّذِي أَرْسَلَهُ اللهُ تَعَالَى رَحْمَةً لِلعَالَمِينَ وَشَفِيعًا لِلْمُذْنِبِينَ

Abtadi'u bi-qawli-l-Lḥamdulillāhi Rabbil ʿĀlamīna wa-ṣ- ***ṣalātu wa-s-salāmu ʿalā Ashrafi-l-Mursalīna*** *Sayyidinā wa Nabiyyinā Muḥammadin wa ʿalā Ālihi wa Ṣaḥbihi ajmaʿīna-l-ladhī arsalahu-Llāhu Taʿālā Raḥmatan li-l-ʿālamīna wa Shafīʿan li-l-mudhnibīna.*
I begin by saying all praises are due to God, the Lord of the worlds, and may peace and salutations be upon the noblest of messengers, our Master and Prophet Muhammad ﷺ, his family and companions entirely, whom God sent as a mercy to all worlds and an intercessor for sinners.

فَيَا سَيِّدِي يَا رَسُوْلَ اللهِ نُنَادِيْكَ مِنْ هَذَا المَكَانِ أَنْ تَنْظُرَ إِلَيْنَا بِنَظْرَةِ الإِحْسَانِ بِنَظْرَةِ مُحِبٍّ فَنَحْنُ وَهَؤُلَاءِ أَحْبَابُكَ يَا رَسُولَ اللهِ ... أَحْبَابُ المُصْطَفَى ... أَحْبَابُ الهُدَى ... أَحْبَابُ الإِسْلَامِ ... أَحْبَابُ النُّورِ ... نُورٌ عَلَى نُورٍ

Fa-yā Sayyidī yā Rasūlallāhi nunādīka min hādhā-l-makāni an tanẓura ilaynā bi-naẓrati-l-iḥsāni bi-naẓrati muḥibbin fa-naḥnu wa hāʾulāʾi aḥbābuka yā Rasūlullāh ... Aḥbābu-l-Muṣṭafā ... Aḥbābu-l-Hudā ... Aḥbābu-l-Islām ... Aḥbābu-n-Nūr ... Nūrun ʿalā Nūr.

Our Master, we call upon you oh Prophet ﷺ from this place, for you to look upon us with the gaze of grace, the gaze of a lover. For we and these are your lovers, oh Messenger of God ﷺ. The lovers of the Chosen One, guidance, Islam and light. Light upon light.

يَا سَيِّدَنَا يَا حَبِيبَنَا يَا رَسُوْلَ اللهِ يَا رَحْمَةً لِلْعَالَمِينَ

Yā Sayyidanā yā Ḥabībanā yā Rasūlallāh yā Raḥmatan li-l-ʿĀlamīna

Oh, our Master, our Beloved, oh Messenger of God ﷺ, oh Mercy to the Worlds.

اللهُمَّ صَلِّ عَلَيْكَ يَا سَيِّدِي يَا رَسُوْلَ اللهِ الَّذِي قُلْتَ فِي حَدِيْثِكَ الشَّرِيْفِ: "إِنَّمَا بُعِثْتُ لِأُتَمِّمَ مَكَارِمَ الأَخْلَاقِ" فَنَرْجُوْا يَا سَيِّدِي يَا رَسُوْلَ اللهِ أَنْ تُتَمِّمَ لَنَا مَكَارِمَ الأَخْلَاقِ

Allāhumma ṣalli ʿalayka yā Sayyidī yā Rasūlullāhi alladhī qulta fī Ḥadīthika ash-Sharīf: "Innamā buʿithtu li-utammima makārima-l-akhlāqi" fa-narjū yā Sayyidī yā Rasūlallāhi an tutammima lanā makārima-l-akhlāq.

May God send His Prayers upon You oh my Master oh Messenger of God ﷺ. You who said that you "were sent only to complete perfect high manners." We hope, our Master, that you will complete our manners.

وَالأَمْرُ بِالصَّلَاةِ عَلَى النَّبِيِّ **صَلَى اللهُ عَلَيْهِ وَسَلَّمَ** يَفِيْضُ عَلَى الحَاضِرِ وَالمُسْتَقْبَلِ وَالمَاضِي فَكُلُّ مَلَكٍ مِنَ المَلَائِكَةِ فَرْضٌ عَلَيْهِ أَنْ يُصَلِّيَ عَلَى النَّبِيِّ **صَلَّى اللهُ عَلَيْهِ وَسَلَّمَ** وَهَذَا فَرْضٌ عَلَيْنَا أَيْضًا أُمَّةُ الحَبِيْبِ المُصْطَفَى **صَلَّى اللهُ عَلَيْهِ وَسَلَّمَ**

Wa-l-amru bi-ṣ-ṣalāti ʿalā-n-Nabiyyi ***ṣallā Allāhu ʿalayhi wa sallama*** *yafīḍu ʿalā-l-ḥāḍiri wa-l-mustaqbali wa-l-māḍī fa-kullu malakin mina-l-malāʾikati farḍun ʿalayhi an yuṣallī ʿalā-n-Nabiyyi* ***ṣallā Allāhu ʿalayhi wa sallam*** *wa hādhā farḍun ʿalaynā ayḍan ummatu-l-Ḥabībi-l-Muṣṭafā* ***ṣallā Allāhu ʿalayhi wa sallam!***

The command to send benedictions on the Prophet ﷺ is timeless, endless and binding on every angel ever created and yet to be created: it applies to the past, present, future and also upon us human beings. All the angels are ordered to make endless benedictions on the Prophet ﷺ, as it is also an obligation on the nation of the Beloved of God ﷺ.

وَيَقُوْلُ سَيِّدِي الحَبِيْبُ عُمَرُ بِنْ مُحَمَّدٍ بِنْ سَالِمِ بِنْ حَفِيْظ حَفِظَهُ اللهُ:

Wa Yaqūlu Sayyidi-l-Ḥabibu Umar bin Muḥammad bin Sālim b. Ḥafīẓ ḥafiẓahu Allāh

Our Master, al-Habib Umar b. Muhammad b. Salim b. Hafidh, God preserve him, says:

وَيَرْوِي الطَبَرَانِيُّ أَنَّ سَيِّدَنَا العَبَّاسُ رَضِيَ اللهُ عَنْهُ نَظَمَ قَصِيْدَةً مَدحَ

النَبِيَّ **صَلَّى اللهُ عَلَيْهِ وَسَلَّمَ** وَقَالَ: يَا رَسُوْلَ اللهِ إِنِّي أُرِيْدُ أَنْ امْتَدِحُكَ. قَالَ لَهُ رَسُوْلُ اللهِ **صَلَّى اللهُ عَلَيْهِ وَسَلَّمَ**: "قُلْ! لَا يَفْضُضْ اللهُ فَاكَ" فَقَالَ:

Wa yarwī aṭ-Ṭabarāniyyu anna sayyidina-l-ʿAbbāsu raḍiya Allāhu ʿanhu naẓama qaṣīdatan madaḥa-n-Nabiyya ***ṣallā Allāhu ʿalayhi wa sallama*** *wa qāla yā Rasūlallāhi innī urīdu an amtadiḥuka. Qāla lahu Rasūlullāhi* ***ṣallā Allāhu ʿalayhi wa sallam:*** *"Qul! Lā yafḍuḍ Allāhu fāka" fa-qāla:*
Al-Tabarani narrates that our master al-ʿAbbas, may God be pleased with him, composed a poem praising the Prophet ﷺ and said: "Oh, Messenger of God, I want to praise you." The Messenger ﷺ said to him: "Say! May God not let your mouth go to ruin." He said:

مِنْ قَبْلِهَا طِبْتَ فِي الظِّلَالِ وَفِي مُسْتَوْدَعٍ حَيْثُ يُخْصَفُ الوَرَقُ

Min qablihā ṭibta fi-ẓ-ẓilāli wa fī mustawdaʿin ḥaythu yukhṣafu-l-waraqu.
Before this you were tranquil, in the shade and a vessel where leaves were used as garment.

ثُمَّ هَبَطْتَ البِلَادَ لَا بَشَرٌ أَنْتَ وَلَا مُضْغَةٌ وَلَا عَلَقُ

Thumma habaṭa-l-bilāda lā basharun anta wa-lā muḍghatun wa-lā ʿalaqu
Then, you descended to the lands, neither as human, clot nor leach.

بَلْ نُطْفَةٌ تَرْكَبُ السَفِيْنَ وَقَدْ أَلْجَمَ نَسْرًا وَأَهْلَهُ الغَرَقُ

Bal nuṭfatun tarkabu-s-safīna wa qad aljama nasran wa ahlahu-l-gharaqu

Rather, a sperm aboard the ark whence the idol Nasr and its people drowned.

تُنْقَلُ مِنْ صَالِبٍ إِلَى رَحِمٍ إِذَا مَضَى عَالَمٌ بَدَا طَبَقُ

Tunqalu min ṣālibin ilā raḥimin idhā maḍā ʿālamun badā ṭabaqu

Moving from loins to wombs. As one world perishes another appears.

وَأَنْتَ لَمَّا وُلِدْتَ أَشْرَقَتْ الأَرْضُ وَاَضَاءَتْ بِنُورِكَ الأُفُقُ

Wa anta lammā wulidta ashraqati-l-arḍu wa aḍāʾat bi-nūrika-l-ufuqu

Then, when you were born, the earth illuminated, and horizons glowed with your light.

فَنَحْنُ فِي ذَلِكَ الضِّيَاءِ وَفِي النُّورِ وَسُبُلِ الرَّشَادِ نَخْتَرِقُ

Fa-naḥnu fī dhālika-ḍ-ḍiyāʾu wa-fi-n-nūri wa subuli-r-rashādi nakhtariqu

And we are in that glow and light, piercing the ways of guidance.

صَدَقْتَ يَا عَبَّاسُ وَنَحْنُ فِي ذَلِكَ الضِّيَاءِ وَفِي النُّوْرِ وَسُبُلِ الرَّشَادِ نَخْتَرِقُ. وَهَلْ عَرَفْنَا لَا إِلَهَ إِلَّا اللهُ إِلَّا بِمُحَمَّدٍ؟ وَهَلْ عَرَفْنَا القُرْآنَ إِلَّا بِمُحَمَّدٍ؟ وَهَلْ عَرَفْنَا الرَّحْمَنَ إِلَّا بِمُحَمَّدٍ **صَلَّى اللهُ عَلَيْهِ وَسَلَّمَ؟**

Ṣadaqta yā ʿAbbāsu wa naḥnu fī dhālika-ḍ-ḍiyāʾu wa fi-n-nūri wa subuli-r-rashādi nakhtariqu. Wa hal ʿarafnā lā ilāha illallāha illā bi-Muḥammadin? Wa hal ʿarafna-l-Qurʾāna illā bi-Muḥammadin? Wa hal ʿarafna-r-Raḥmāna illā bi-Muḥammadin ***ṣallā Allāhu ʿalayhi wa sallam?***

You are truthful, oh Abbas. Indeed, we are in that glow and light piercing the ways of guidance. For did we come to know 'There is no god but God save through Muhammad ﷺ? Did we come to know the Qur'an save through Muhammad ﷺ? Did we come to know the Most-Merciful save through Muhammad ﷺ?

فَجَزَاهُ اللهُ عَنَّا خَيْرًا أَفْضَلَ مَا جَازَى نَبِيًّا عَنْ أُمَّتِهِ وَحَشَرَنَا جَمِيْعًا فِي زُمْرَتِه. وَمَحَبَّةُ النَّبِيِّ **صَلَّى اللهُ عَلَيْهِ وَسَلَّمَ** مَعَ مَحَبَّةِ الحَقِّ عَزَّ وَجَلَّ فِي القُرْآنِ وَالسُّنَّةِ لَا يَتَفَرَّقَا وَغَيْرُ مَحْدُودَةٍ أَبَدًا. فَلَا يُمْكِنُ أَنْ يَكُونَ شَيْئًا أَحَبُّ إِلَيْنَا مِنْ هَذَا الرَّسُولِ بَعْدَ اللهِ عَزَّ وَجَلَّ.

*Fa-jazāhu Allāhu ʿannā khayrin afḍala mā jāzā nabiyyan ʿan ummatihi wa ḥasharana jamīʿan fī zumratih. Wa maḥabbatu-n-Nabiyyi **ṣallā Allāhu ʿalayhi wa sallama** maʿa maḥabbati-l-Ḥaqqi ʿazza wa jalla fi-l-Qurʾani wa-s-sunnati lā yatafarraqā wa ghayru maḥdūdatin abadan. Fa-lā yumkinu an yakūna shayʾan aḥabbu ilaynā min hādha-r-Rasūli baʿda Allāhi ʿazza wa jalla.*

So, may God reward him ﷺ on our behalf the best of rewards and of what He has rewarded a prophet on behalf of his people. May He resurrect us together with him. And the love of the Prophet ﷺ is tethered to the love of the Real, may He be exalted, in the Qur'an and Sunna. They never separate nor are they bounded by a limit. So, it is not possible for anyone or anything to be more beloved to us, after God, may He be exalted, than this Messenger ﷺ.

اللهُمَّ صَلِّ وَسَلِّمْ وَبَارِكْ عَلَيْهِ وَعَلَى آلِهْ

Allāhumma ṣalli wa sallim wa bārik ʿalayhi wa ʿalā ālih

Oh God, send your prayers, salutations and blessings, upon Him and His Family.

بِسْمِ اللَّهِ الرَّحْمَٰنِ الرَّحِيمِ

Bismillāhi-r-Raḥmāni-r-Raḥīm
In the Name of God, Most Beneficent Most Merciful

الفَصْلُ الثَّاني:
مُقَدِّمَة

Al-Faṣlu-th-Thānī: Muqaddimah
Chapter Two: Introduction

يَا رَبِّ صَلِّ عَلَى مُحَمَّدْ   مِنْهُ فِيهِ عَلَيْنَا سَرْمَدَا

Yā Rabbi ṣalli ʿalā Muḥammad
Minhu fīhi ʿalaynā sarmadā
My Lord send your prayers upon Muhammad,
Bestow, through him, upon us eternally.

يَا رَبِّ صَلِّ عَلَى مُحَمَّدْ   بِهِ طَلْعَةُ الذَّاتِ الْمُطَلْسَمْ

Yā Rabbi ṣalli ʿalā Muḥammad
Bihi ṭalʿatu-dh-dhāti-l-Muṭalsam
My Lord send your prayers upon Muhammad,
In whom is the appearance of the Concealed Essence.

يَا رَبِّ صَلِّ عَلَى مُحَمَّدْ   وَحَقِيْقَةُ الغَيْثِ الْمُطَمْطَمْ

Yā Rabbi ṣalli ʿalā Muḥammad
Wa ḥaqīqatu-l-Ghaythi-l-Muṭamṭam
My Lord send your prayers upon Muhammad,
The reality of the Overflowing Succor.

يَا رَبِّ صَلِّ عَلَى مُحَمَّدْ   وَبَهْجَةُ الكَمَالِ الْمُكْتَتَمْ

Yā Rabbi ṣalli ʿalā Muḥammad

Wa bahjatu-l-Kamāli-l-Muktatam
My Lord send your prayers upon Muhammad,
The splendor of the Hidden Perfection.

يَا رَبِّ صَلِّ عَلَى مُحَمَّدْ فِيْهِ جَوْهَرُ لَاهُوْتِ الجَمَالْ

Yā Rabbi ṣalli ʿalā Muḥammad
Fīhi jawharu Lāhūti-l-Jamāl
My Lord send your prayers upon Muhammad,
In whom is the jewel of Divine Beauty.

يَا رَبِّ صَلِّ عَلَى مُحَمَّدْ مِنْهُ لُؤْلُؤُ نَاسُوْتِ الوِصَالْ

Yā Rabbi ṣalli ʿalā Muḥammad
Minhu Luʾluʾu Nāsūti-l-Wiṣāl
My Lord send your prayers upon Muhammad,
From whom emerges the pearl of God's Intimacy.

يَا رَبِّ صَلِّ عَلَى مُحَمَّدْ فِيْهِ حَقِيْقَةُ طَلْعَةِ الحَقّ

Yā Rabbi ṣalli ʿalā Muḥammad
Fīhi ḥaqīqatu Ṭalʿati-l-Ḥaqq
My Lord send your prayers upon Muhammad,
In whom is the reality of the appearance of the Real.

يَا رَبِّ صَلِّ عَلَى مُحَمَّدْ وَهُوِيَّةُ إِنْسَانِ الأَزَلْ

Yā Rabbi ṣalli ʿalā Muḥammad
Wa huwiyyatu Insāni-l-Azal
My Lord send your prayers upon Muhammad,
The identity of the primordial human.

يَا رَبِّ صَلِّ عَلَى مُحَمَّدْ يَا مَنْ فِيهِ نَشْرُ مَنْ لَمْ يَزَلْ

Yā Rabbi ṣalli ʿalā Muḥammad
Ya man fīhi nashru man lam yazal

My Lord send your prayers upon Muhammad,
In whom is the dispersion of the One who subsists.

يَا رَبِّ صَلِّ عَلَى مُحَمَّدْ وَإِقَامَةُ نَاسُوْتِ الفِرَقْ

Yā Rabbi ṣalli ʿalā Muḥammad
Wa iqāmatu nāsūti-l-firaq
My Lord send your prayers upon Muhammad,
Through whom stands the principle of Divine Multiplicity.

يَا رَبِّ صَلِّ عَلَى مُحَمَّدْ بِهِ عَيْنُ الطَّرِيْقِ إِلَى الحَقّ

Yā Rabbi ṣalli ʿalā Muḥammad
Bihi ʿAynu-ṭ-Ṭarīqi ilā-l-Ḥaqq
My Lord send your prayers upon Muhammad,
Through whom is the essence of the path to the Real.

يَا رَبِّ صَلِّ عَلَى مُحَمَّدْ مِنْهُ فِيْهِ عَلَيْنَا سَرْمَدَا

Yā Rabbi ṣalli ʿalā Muḥammad
Minhu fīhi ʿalaynā sarmadā
My Lord send your prayers upon Muhammad,
Bestow, through him, upon us eternally.

اللهُمَّ صَلِّ وَسَلِّمْ وَبَارِكْ عَلَيْهِ وَعَلَى آلِهْ

Allāhumma ṣalli wa sallim wa bārik ʿalayhi wa ʿalā ālih
Oh God, send your prayers, salutations and blessings, upon Him and His Family.

بِسْمِ اللَّهِ الرَّحْمَٰنِ الرَّحِيمِ

Bismillāhi-r-Raḥmāni-r-Raḥīm
In the Name of God, Most Beneficent Most Merciful

الفَصْلُ الثَّالِثُ:
القُرْآنُ الكَرِيم

Al-Faṣlu-th-Thālith: Al-Qur'ānu-l-Karīm
Chapter Three: Holy Qur'an

﴿إِنَّا فَتَحْنَا لَكَ فَتْحًا مُبِينًا﴾ (٤٨:١)

*Innā **fataḥnā** laka **fatḥan** mubīnā* (48:1)
"We have **opened** for you a vivid **opening**" (48:1)

﴿فَتْحٌ مِنَ اللهِ وَنَصْرٌ قَرِيبٌ وَبَشِّرِ الْمُؤْمِنِيْنَ﴾ (٦١:١٣)

Fatḥun** min Allāhi wa naṣrun qarībun wa bashshiri-l-**mu'minīn (61:13)
"An **opening** from God, near victory and give glad tidings to the **believers**" (61:13)

﴿لَقَدْ مَنَّ اللهُ عَلَى الْمُؤْمِنِيْنَ إِذْ بَعَثَ فِيْهِمْ رَسُوْلًا مِنْ أَنْفُسِهِمْ﴾

(٣:١٦٤)

*Laqad manna Allāhu 'alā-l-**mu'minīna** idh ba'atha fīhim Rasūlan min anfusihim* (3:164)
"God has bestowed His bounty upon the **believers**, when He sent them a messenger from within their own selves" (3:164)

﴿لَقَدْ جَاءَكُمْ مِنَ اللهِ نُوْرٌ وَكِتَابٌ مُبِيْنٌ﴾ (٥:١٥)

Laqad jā'akum min Allāhi
Nūrun** wa **Kitābun Munīr (5:15)
"Indeed, there has come to you from God a **light** and **clear book**" (5:15)

﴿يَا أَيُّهَا **النَّبِيُّ** إِنَّا أَرْسَلْنَاكَ شَاهِدًا وَمُبَشِّرًا وَنَذِيرًا ۞ وَدَاعِيًا إِلَى اللهِ بِإِذْنِهِ **وَسِرَاجًا مُنِيرًا**﴾ (٣٣:٤٥)

*Yā ayyuhā-n-**Nabiyyu** Innā arsalnāka Shāhidan wa Mubashshiran wa Nadhīra wa Dā'iyan ilā Allāhi bi-idhnihi wa **Sirājan Munīra*** (33:45-46)
"Oh **Prophet**, We have sent you as a witness, giver of glad tidings, warner, caller to God through His permission and a **glowing lamp**" (33:45-46)

﴿اللهُ **نُورُ** السَّمَاوَاتِ وَالأَرْضِ مَثَلُ **نُورِهِ** كَمِشْكَاةٍ فِيهَا مِصْبَاحٌ الْمِصْبَاحُ فِي زُجَاجَةٍ الزُّجَاجَةُ كَأَنَّهَا كَوْكَبٌ دُرِّيٌّ يُوقَدُ مِنْ شَجَرَةٍ مُبَارَكَةٍ زَيْتُونَةٍ لَا شَرْقِيَّةٍ وَلَا غَرْبِيَّةٍ يَكَادُ زَيْتُهَا يُضِيءُ وَلَوْ لَمْ تَمْسَسْهُ نَارٌ **نُورٌ** عَلَى **نُورٍ** يَهْدِي اللهُ **لِنُورِهِ** مَنْ يَشَاءُ وَيَضْرِبُ اللهُ الأَمْثَالَ لِلنَّاسِ وَاللهُ بِكُلِّ شَيْءٍ عَلِيمٌ﴾ (٢٤:٣٥)

*Allāhu **Nūru**-s-samāwāti wa-l-arḍi mathalu **Nūrihi** ka-mishkātin fīhā miṣbāḥun al-miṣbāḥu fī zujājatin az-zujājatu ka-annahā kawkabun durriyyun yūqadu min shajaratin mubārakatin zaytūnatin lā sharqiyyatin wa lā gharbiyyatin yakādu zaytuhā yuḍī'u wa law lam tamsashu nārun **Nūrun** 'alā **Nūrin** yahdi-Llāhu li-**Nūrihi** man yashā'u wa yaḍribu-Llāhu-l-amthāla li-n-nāsi wa-Allāhu bi-kulli shay'in 'Alīm* (24:35)
"Indeed, God is the **Light** of the Heavens and Earth. The example of **His Light** is like a niche within which is a

lamp. The lamp resides in a glass case. The glass case is like a glowing star ignited from a blessed olive tree, neither easterly nor westerly. Its light sparks without fire touching it. **Light** upon **light**! Indeed, God guides to **His Light** whomever He wills. God provides parables for people and God knows all things." (24:35)

﴿اهْدِنَا الصِّرَاطَ الْمُسْتَقِيمْ﴾ (١:٦)

﴿وَإِنَّكَ لَتَهْدِي إِلَى صِرَاطٍ مُسْتَقِيمْ﴾ (٤٢:٥٢)

﴿وَأَنَّ هَذَا صِرَاطِي مُسْتَقِيمًا فَاتَّبِعُوهُ﴾ (٦:١٥٣)

Ihdina-ṣ-ṣirāṭa-l-mustaqīm (1:6)
*Wa Innaka la-**tahdī** ilā **ṣirāṭin mustaqīm*** (42:52)
*Wa anna hādhā **Ṣirāṭī Mustaqīman** fa-t-tabiʿūh* (6:153)
"Guide us to the **right path**" (1:6)
"You **guide** to the **right path**" (42:52)
"Indeed, this is **my path**, it is **right**, so follow it!" (6:153)

﴿هُوَ الَّذِي يُصَلِّي عَلَيْكُمْ وَمَلَائِكَتُهُ لِيُخْرِجَكُمْ مِنَ الظُّلُمَاتِ إِلَى النُّوْرِ وَكَانَ بِالْمُؤْمِنِينَ رَحِيمًا ۞ تَحِيَّتُهُمْ يَوْمَ يَلْقَوْنَهُ سَلَامٌ وَأَعَدَّ لَهُمْ أَجْرًا كَرِيمًا﴾ (٣٣:٤٣)

*Huwa-l-ladhī **yuṣallī** ʿalaykum wa malāʾikatuhu li-yukhrijakum min-ẓ-ẓulumāti ila-n-nūr wa kāna bi-l-muʾminīna Raḥīma. Taḥiyyatuhum yawma yalqawnahu **salāmun** wa aʿadda lahum ajran karīma* (33:34-44)
"He is the One who **prays** upon you and His angels as well, in order to take you from the darknesses to the light. Indeed, He is Most-Merciful with the believers. Their greeting on the day they see Him is '**peace**!' and He has prepared for them a generous reward" (33:43-44)

﴿سَلَامٌ قَوْلًا مِنْ رَبٍّ رَحِيمٍ﴾ (٣٦:٥٨)

***Salāmun** qawlan min Rabbi-r-Raḥīm* (36:58)
"A **peaceful greeting of peace** from a merciful caretaker/Lord" (36:58)

﴿إِنَّ اللهَ وَمَلَائِكَتَهُ **يُصَلُّوْنَ** عَلَى **النَّبِيِّ** يَا أَيُّهَا الَّذِيْنَ آمَنُوْا **صَلُّوْا** عَلَيْهِ وَسَلِّمُوْا تَسْلِيمًا﴾ (٣٣:٥٦)

*Inna Allāha wa malāʾikatahu **yuṣallūna** ʿala-n-**Nabiyyi** yā ayyuha-l-ladhīna āmanū **ṣallū** ʿalayhi wa **sallimū taslīmā***
"Indeed, God and His angels **send prayers** upon the **Prophet**. Oh, you who believe **send prayers** upon Him and **abundant salutations**" (33:56)

اللهُمَّ صَلِّ وَسَلِّمْ وَبَارِكْ عَلَيْهِ وَعَلَى آلِهْ

Allāhumma ṣalli wa sallim wa bārik ʿalayhi wa ʿalā ālih
Oh God, send your prayers, salutations and blessings, upon Him and His Family.

بِسْمِ اللَّهِ الرَّحْمَٰنِ الرَّحِيمِ

Bismillāhi-r-Raḥmāni-r-Raḥīm

In the Name of God, Most Beneficent Most Merciful

الفَصْلُ الرَّابِعُ: التَّعْرِيْفُ بِمَقَامِهِ العَلِيِّ ﷺ

Al-Faṣlu-r-Rābiʿ: At-Taʿrīf bi Maqāmihi-l-ʿAliyyi ṣallā Allāhu ʿalayhi wa sallam

Chapter Four: Informing of His Lofty Rank ﷺ

أَمَّا بَعْدُ، فَيَقُوْلُ سَيِّدِي الشَّيْخُ الأَكْبَرُ وَالكِبْرِيْتُ الأَحْمَرُ مُحْيِي الدِّيْنِ ابْنُ العَرَبِيُّ الحَاتِمِيُّ الطَّائِيُّ قَدَّسَ اللهُ سِرَّهُ: "الحَمْدُ للهِ مُنْزِلِ الحِكَمِ عَلَى قُلُوْبِ الكَلِمِ بِأَحَدِيَّةِ الطَّرِيقِ الأَمِمِ مِنَ المَقَامِ الأَقْدَمِ وَإِنْ اخْتَلَفَتْ النِّحَلُ وَالمِلَلُ لِاخْتِلَافِ الأُمَمْ. وَصَلَّى اللهُ عَلَى مُمِدِّ الهِمَمِ مِنْ خَزَائِنِ الجُوْدِ وَالكَرَمِ وَبِالْقِيْلِ الأَقْوَمْ، سَيِّدِنَا مُحَمَّدٍ **صَلَّى اللهُ عَلَيْهِ وَسَلَّمْ**.

Ammā baʿdu, fa-yaqūlu sayyidi-sh-Shaykhu-l-Akbaru wa-l-Kibrītu-l-Aḥmaru Muḥyi-d-Dīni Ibnu-l-ʿArabiyyu-l-Ḥātimiyyu-t-Ṭāʾī qaddasa Allāhu sirrahu: "Alḥamdulillāhi munzili-l-ḥikami ʿalā qulūbi-l-Kalimi bi-aḥadiyati-ṭ-ṭarīqi-l-amimi mina-l-maqāmi-l-aqdami wa in-i-khtalafati-l-niḥalu wa-l-milalu li-khtilāfi-l-umam. Wa ṣallā Allāhu ʿalā mumiddi-l-himami min khazāʾini-l-jūdi wa-l-karami bi-l-qīli-l-aqwam, Sayyidinā Muḥammadin ***ṣallā Allāhu ʿalayhi wa sallam****.*

Our teacher, the Greatest Master and Red Sulfur, Muhyi al-Din Ibn al-ʿArabi, God sanctify his secret, says: "All praise is due to God who cast wisdoms upon the hearts of His Words, through the singularity of the nearest path, from the pre-eternal ancient station, despite the differences between sects and groups due to the variety of nations. And **may God send His prayers upon the one** who sustains determinations from the treasuries of bounty and generosity with the most upright speech, our Master Muḥammad ﷺ.

إِنَّمَا كَانَتْ حِكْمَتُهُ فَرْدِيَّةٌ **صَلَّى اللهُ عَلَيْهِ وَسَلَّمَ** لِأَنَّهُ أَكْمَلُ مَوْجُوْدٍ فِي هَذَا النَّوْعِ الإِنْسَانِي، وَلِهَذَا بُدِئَ بِهِ الأَمْرُ وَخُتِمْ: فَكَانَ نَبِيًّا وَآدَمُ بَيْنَ المَاءِ وَالطِّينِ، ثُمَّ كَانَ بِنَشْأَتِهِ العُنْصُرِّيَةِ خَاتَمَ النَبِيِّينَ، **صَلَّى اللهُ عَلَيْهِ وَسَلَّمْ.**

Innamā kānat ḥikmatuhu fardiyyatun ***ṣallā Allāhu ʿalayhi wa sallama*** *li-annahu akmalu mawjūdin fī hādha-n-nawʿi-l-insānī, wa li-hādhā budiʾa bihi-l-amru wa khutim: fa-kāna nabiyyan wa Adāmu bayna-l-māʾi wa-ṭ-ṭīn. Thumma kāna bi-nashʾatihi-l-ʿunṣriyyati Khātama-n-nabiyyinā,* ***ṣallā Allāhu ʿalayhi wa sallam!***

His wisdom ﷺ is singular and unique and he is the most perfect being among the human species. This is why creation began and is sealed with him ﷺ. He was a prophet while Adam was still between water and clay. Thus, even in His elemental composition, he is the seal of prophets ﷺ.

وَكَانَ **صَلَّى اللهُ عَلَيْهِ وَسَلَّمَ** مُبْتَدَأَ وُجُوْدِ العَالَمِ عَقْلًا وَنَفْسًا "مَتَى كُنْتَ نَبِيًّا" قَالَ "وَآدَمُ بَيْنَ المَاءِ وَالطِّينِ" فَبِهِ بُدِئَ الوُجُوْدِ بَاطِنًا وَبِهِ خُتِمَ المَقَامُ ظَاهِرًا فِي عَالَمِ التَّخْطِيْطِ فَقَالَ "لَا رَسُولَ بَعْدِي وَلَا نَبِيٌّ"، **صَلَّى اللهُ عَلَيْهِ وَسَلَّمْ.**

Wa kāna ***ṣallā Allāhu ʿalayhi wa sallama*** *mubtadaʾa wujūdi-l-ʿālami ʿaqlan wa nafsan. "Matā kunta nabiyyan?" qāla "Wa Ādamu bayna-l-māʾi wa-ṭ-ṭīn." Fa-bihi budiʾa-l-wujūdu bāṭinan wa bihi khutima-l-maqāmu ẓāhiran fī ʿālami-ṭ-ṭakhṭīṭi fa-qāla "la rasūla baʿdī wa lā nabiyyun",* ***ṣallā Allāhu ʿalayhi wa sallam!***

And he ﷺ is the beginning of existence of the world, intellectually and spiritually. "When were You a Prophet?" He said: "While Adam was still between water and clay." Thus, through him existence began inwardly and through him the station is sealed outwardly in the world of divine plans. He said: "There is neither messenger nor prophet after me," ﷺ.

فَكُلُّ نَبِيٍّ مِنْ لَدُنْ آدَمَ إِلَى آخِرِ نَبِيٍّ مَا مِنْهُمْ أَحَدٌ يَأْخُذُ إِلَّا مِنْ مِشْكَاةِ خَاتَمِ النَّبِيِّينَ، وَإِنْ تَأَخَّرَ وُجُودُ طِينَتِهِ، فَإِنَّهُ بِحَقِيقَتِهِ مَوْجُودٌ، وَهُوَ قَوْلُهُ **صَلَّى اللهُ عَلَيْهِ وَسَلَّمَ**: «كُنْتُ نَبِيًّا وَآدَمُ بَيْنَ المَاءِ وَالطِّينِ». وَغَيْرُهُ مِنَ الأَنْبِيَاءِ مَا كَانَ نَبِيًّا إِلَّا حِينَ بُعِثَ **صَلَّى اللهُ عَلَيْهِ وَسَلَّمْ**.

Fa kullu nabiyyin min ladun Ādama ilā ākhiri nabiyyin mā minhum aḥadun yaʾkhudhu illā min mishkāti Khātami-n-Nabiyyīn, wa in taʾkhkhara wujūdu ṭīnatihi, fa-innahu bi ḥaqīqatihi mawjūdun, wa huwa qawluhu ***ṣallā Allāhu ʿalayhi wa sallama****: "Kuntu Nabiyyan wa Ādamu bayna-l-māʾi wa-ṭ-ṭīn" wa ghayrihu mina-l-anbiyāʾi mā kāna nabiyyan illā ḥīna buʿitha* ***ṣallā Allāhu ʿalayhi wa sallam.***

Thus, every prophet, from the time of Adam to the last Prophet, none of them receives any knowledge except from the niche of the seal of prophets ﷺ, even though the emergence of his body was delayed. This is because he existed in his reality ﷺ. This is proven by his statement ﷺ: "I was a prophet while Adam was still between water and clay." Meanwhile, prophets other than him only receive this rank when they are sent as such. **May God's Prayers and Salutations be upon Him**.

فَكَانَ **صَلَّى اللهُ عَلَيْهِ وَسَلَّمَ** أَدَلُّ دَلِيْلٍ عَلَى رَبِّهِ، فَإِنَّهُ أُوْتِيَ جَوَامِعَ الكَلِمِ الَّتِي هِيَ مُسَمَّيَاتُ أَسْمَاءِ آدَمَ عَلَيْهِ السَّلَامْ، فَعَلَّمَهُ اللهُ مَا لَمْ يَكُنْ يَعْلَمُ وَكَانَ فَضْلُ اللهِ عَلَيْهِ عَظِيمًا. فَمَا أَعْلَمَهُ **صَلَّى اللهُ عَلَيْهِ وَسَلَّمَ** بِالحَقَائِقِ وَمَا أَشَدَّ رِعَايَتِهِ لِلحُقُوْقِ، **صَلَّى اللهُ عَلَيْهِ وَسَلَّمْ**.

Fa-kāna ***ṣallā Allāhu ʿalayhi wa sallama*** *adallu dalīlin ʿalā Rabbihi, fa-innahu ūtiya jawāmiʿi-l-kalimi allatī hiya musammayātu asmāʾi Ādama ʿalayhi-s-salām, fa-ʿallamahu-Llāhu mā lam yakun yaʿlam wa kāna faḍlu-Llāhi ʿalayhi ʿaẓīma. Fa-mā aʿlamahu* ***ṣallā Allāhu ʿalayhi wa sallam*** *bi-l-ḥaqāʾiqi wa mā ashadda riʿāyatihi li-l-ḥuqūq,* ***ṣallā Allāhu ʿalayhi wa sallam****.*

He ﷺ is the clearest proof of his Lord, for He was given the most encompassing speech which are the meanings of the names granted to Adam ﵇. In this way, God ﷻ taught him what he did not know and His bounty upon him was immense. So, contemplate how much knowledge he ﷺ has of spiritual realities and the care he gives towards the rights of others, ﷺ.

فَلَمْ يَكُنْ أَحَدٌ أَكْمَلُ مِنْ رَسُوْلِ اللهِ **صَلَّى اللهُ عَلَيْهِ وَسَلَّمَ** وَلَا أَعْلَى وَلَا أَقْوَى هِمَّةً مِنْهُ. فَفَازَ مُحَمَّدٌ **صَلَّى اللهُ عَلَيْهِ وَسَلَّمَ** بِالسِّيَادَةِ فِي هَذَا المَقَامِ الخَاصْ. فَمَنْ فَهِمَ المَرَاتِبَ وَالمَقَامَاتِ لَمْ يَعْسُرْ عَلَيْهِ قَبُوْلَ مِثْلَ هَذَا الكَلَامِ **صَلَّى اللهُ عَلَيْهِ وَسَلَّمْ**.

Fa-lam yakun aḥadun akmalu min Rasūli Allāhi ***ṣallā Allāhu ʿalayhi wa sallam*** *wa lā aʿlā wa lā aqwā himmatin* *minhu. Fa-fāza Muḥammadun* ***ṣallā Allāhu ʿalayhi wa sallama*** *bi-s-siyādati fī hādha-l-maqāmi-l-khāṣ. Fa-man fahima-l-marātiba wa-l-maqāmāti lam yaʿsur ʿalayhi qabūla mithla hādha-l-kalāmi,* ***ṣallā Allāhu ʿalayhi wa sallam.***

Indeed, no one is more perfect, loftier in rank or stronger in determination than the Messenger of God ﷺ. In this way, Muhammad ﷺ reached mastery in this special station. Whoever understands degrees and spiritual stations will not have difficulty accepting our speech, ﷺ.

فَإِنْ نَظَرْنَا إِلَى سِيَادَتِهِ عَلَى جَمِيعِ مَا سِوَى الحَقِّ فَإِنَّهُ كَمَا ذَهَبَ إِلَيْهِ بَعْضُ النَّاسِ لِلحَدِيْثِ المَرْوِيِّ أَنَّ اللهَ يَقُوْلُ "لَوْلَاكَ يَا مُحَمَّدًا مَا خَلَقْتُ سَمَاءً وَلَا أَرْضًا وَلَا جَنَّةً وَلَا نَارًا" وَذَكَرَ خَلْقَ كُلِّ مَا سِوَى اللهِ **صَلَّى اللهُ عَلَيْهِ وَسَلَّمْ.**

Fa-in naẓarnā ilā siyādatihi ʿalā jamīʿi mā siwa-l-Ḥaqqi, fa innahu ka-mā dhahaba ilayhi baʿḍu-n-nāsi li-l-ḥadīthi al-marwiyyi anna Allāha yaqūlu: "law-lāka yā Muḥammadan mā khalaqtu samāʾan wa-lā arḍan wa-lā jannatan wa-lā nāran" wa dhakara khalqa kulli mā siwā Allāhi, ***ṣallā Allāhu ʿalayhi wa sallam.***

If we contemplate his mastery ﷺ upon everything other than the Real ﷻ, then reality is as some people have narrated, that God ﷻ has said: "If it were not for you Muhammad, I would have created neither heaven, earth, paradise nor hell," and He continues to mention all the creation other than Himself, ﷺ.

فَأَيُّ شَرَفٍ أَعْظَمُ مِنْ شَرَفِ مُحَمَّدٍ **صَلَّى اللهُ عَلَيْهِ وَسَلَّمَ** حَيْثُ كَانَ

ابْتِدَاءَ هَذِهِ الدَّائِرَةِ حَيْثُ اتَّصَلَ بِهَا آخِرُهَا لِكَمَالِهَا فَبِهِ **صَلَّى اللهُ عَلَيْهِ وَسَلَّمَ** ابْتَدَأَتْ الأَشْيَاءُ وَبِهِ كَمُلَتْ وَمَا أَعْظَمُ شَرَفَ الْمُؤْمِنِ حَيْثُ نِلْتَ شَفَاعَتَهُ بِشَفَاعَةِ أَرْحَمِ الرَّاحِمِيْنَ فَالْمُؤْمِنُ بَيْنَ اللهِ والأَنْبِيَاءِ، **صَلَّى اللهُ عَلَيْهِ وَسَلَّمْ.**

Fa-ayyu sharafin aʿẓamu min sharafi Muḥammadin ***ṣallā Allāhu ʿalayhi wa sallama*** *ḥaythu kāna ibtidāʾa hādhihi-d-dāʾirati ḥaythu ittaṣala bihā ākhiruhā li-kamālihā fa-bihi* ***ṣallā Allāhu ʿalayhi wa sallama*** *ibtadaʾati-l-ashyāʾu wa bihi kamulat wa mā aʿẓamu sharafi-l-muʾmini ḥaythu nilta shafāʿatahu bi-shafāʿati Arḥami-r-Rāḥimīna fa-l-muʾminu bayna Allāhi wa-l-anbiyāʾ,* ***ṣallā Allāhu ʿalayhi wa sallam.***
What honor is more greater than that of Muhammad ﷺ, for he was the beginning of this circle of creation and prophecy, whence he also became connected to its end. Thus, it was perfected. Through him ﷺ things emerged and through him they were perfected. How great then is the honor of the believer. You have been rewarded with his intercession ﷺ, as a result of the Intercession of the Most-Merciful of the merciful ones. Indeed, the believer resides between God and His prophets ﷺ.

فَلَا فُلْكَ أَوْسَعُ مِنْ فُلْكِ مُحَمَّدٍ **صَلَّى اللهُ عَلَيْهِ وَسَلَّمَ** فَإِنَّ لَهُ الإِحَاطَةُ وَهِيَ لِمَنْ خَصَّهُ اللهُ بِهَا مِنْ أُمَّتِهِ بِحُكْمِ التَّبَعِيَّةِ فَلَنَا الإِحَاطَةُ بِسَائِرِ الأُمَمِ وَلِذَلِكَ كُنَّا شُهَدَاءَ عَلَى النَّاسِ فَأَعْطَاهُ اللهُ مِنْ وَحْيِ أَمْرِ السَّمَاوَاتِ مَا لَمْ يُعْطِ غَيْرَهُ **صَلَّى اللهُ عَلَيْهِ وَسَلَّم.**

Fa-lā fulka awsaʿu min fulki Muḥammadin ***ṣallā Allāhu ʿalayhi wa sallama*** *fa-inna lahu-l-iḥāṭatu wa hiya li-man khaṣṣahu Allāhu bihā min ummatihi bi-ḥukmi-t-tabaʿiyyati* *fa-lanā-l-iḥāṭatu bi-sāʾiri-l-umami wa li-dhālika kunnā shuhadāʾa ʿala-n-nāsi fa-aʿṭāhu Allāhu min waḥiy amri-s-samāwāti mā lam yuʿṭi ghayrahu **ṣallā Allāhu ʿalayhi wa sallam**.*

There is no orbit more expansive than that of Muhammad ﷺ. Indeed, he has the encompassment which is also granted to whomever God ﷻ Wills from among his community, as a reward for following him ﷺ. This is why we have been granted knowledge encompassing other nations and have been made as witnesses upon them. Indeed, God ﷻ has revealed to him ﷺ the affairs of heavenly commands that He has not granted to anyone else, ﷺ.

وَمِنَ اللهِ أَرْجُوْ أَنْ أَكُوْنَ مِمَّنْ أُيِّدَ فَتَأَيَّدَ وَقُيِّدَ بِالشَّرْعِ الْمُحَمَّدِيِّ الْمُطَهَّرِ فَتَقَيَّدَ وَقَيَّدْ، وَحَشَرَنَا فِي زُمْرَتِهِ كَمَا جَعَلَنَا مِنْ أُمَّتِهِ **صَلَّى اللهُ عَلَيْهِ وَسَلَّم**.

*Wa mina Allāhi arjū an akūna mimman uyyida fa-taʾyyada wa quiyyida bi-sh-sharʿi-l-Muḥammadiyyi al-muṭahhari fa-taqayyada wa qayyad, wa ḥasharana fī zumratihi ka-mā jaʿalanā min ummatihi **ṣallā Allāhu ʿalayhi wa sallam**.*

I ask God ﷻ to be from among those who are given Divine Aid, become affirmed and confined to the purified Muhammadan law; to become obedient and established in his way as such. And may God ﷻ gather us together in his group just as he has made us from his community ﷺ.

اللهُمَّ صَلِّ وَسَلِّمْ وَبَارِكْ عَلَيْهِ وَعَلَى آلِهْ

Allāhumma ṣalli wa sallim wa bārik ʿalayhi wa ʿalā ālih

Oh God, send your Prayers, Salutations and Blessings, upon Him and His Family.

بِسْمِ اللَّهِ الرَّحْمَنِ الرَّحِيمِ

Bismillāhi-r-Raḥmāni-r-Raḥīm
In the Name of God, Most Beneficent Most Merciful

الفَصْلُ الخَامِسُ: حَقِيْقَةُ وَصْفِ خَلْقِهِ ﷺ وَكَوْنِهِ مَظْهَرُ حَقَايِقِ كَلَامِ اللهِ ﷻ

Al-Faṣlu-l-Khāmis: Ḥaqīqatu Waṣfi Khalqihi ﷺ Wa Kawnihi Maẓharu Ḥaqāʾiqi Kalāmi Allāhi ﷻ

Chapter Five: His Reality ﷺ as a Walking Qurʾan

قَالَ اللهُ تَعَالَى ﴿وَإِنَّكَ لَعَلَى خُلُقٍ عَظِيمٍ﴾ (٦٨:٤) وَلَمَّا سُئِلَتْ عَائِشَةُ رَضِيَ اللهُ عَنْهَا عَنْ خُلُقِ رَسُوْلِ اللهِ **صَلَّى اللهُ عَلَيْهِ وَسَلَّمَ** قَالَتْ "كَانَ خُلُقُهُ القُرْآنَ" وَإِنَّمَا قَالَتْ ذَلِكَ لِأَنَّهُ أَفْرَدُ الخَلْقِ وَلَابُدَّ أَنْ يَكُوْنَ ذَلِكَ الخَلْقُ المُفْرَدُ جَامِعًا لِمَكَارِمِ الأَخْلَاقِ كُلِّهَا.

*Qāla Allāhu Taʿālā: "Wa innaka la-ʿalā khuluqin ʿaẓīm". Wa lammā suʾilat ʿĀʾisha raḍiya Allāhu ʿanhā ʿan khuluqi Rasūlillāhi **ṣallā Allāhu ʿalayhi wa sallama** qālat: "Kāna khuluquhu-l-Qurʾān" wa innamā qālat dhālika li-annahu afradu-l-khalqi wa lā budda an yakūna dhālika-l-khalqu-l-mufradu jāmiʿan li-makārimi-l-akhlāqi kullihā.*

God ﷻ said: "Indeed, You are upon Great Character" (68:4)

And when ʿAʾisha ؓ was asked about the character of the Messenger of God ﷺ she said: "His character is the Qurʾan". She said this because he is the most unique among all creation, and a singular one as such must encompass all the perfected traits.

وَوَصَفَ اللهُ ذَلِكَ الخُلُقَ بِالعَظَمَةِ كَمَا وَصَفَ القُرْآنَ فِي قَوْلِهِ ﴿وَالقُرْآنَ العَظِيمِ﴾ (١٥:٨٧) فَكَانَ القُرْآنَ خُلُقُهُ **صَلَّى اللهُ عَلَيْهِ وَسَلَّمْ**.

Wa waṣafa Allāhu dhālika-l-khalqu bi-l-ʿaẓamati ka-mā waṣafa-l-Qurʾāna fī qawlihi "Wa-l-Qurʾāna-l-ʿAẓīm" fa-kāna-l-Qurʾānu khuluquhu ***ṣallā Allāhu ʿalayhi wa sallam.***

God ﷻ has also described his creation ﷺ with greatness, just as He described the Qurʾan in His statement: "And the Great Qurʾan" (15:87). In this way, the Qurʾan is his character, ﷺ.

فَمَنْ أَرَادَ أَنْ يَرَى رَسُوْلَ اللهِ **صَلَّى اللهُ عَلَيْهِ وَسَلَّمَ** مِمَّنْ لَمْ يُدْرِكْهُ مِنْ أُمَّتِهِ فَلْيَنْظُرْ إِلَى القُرْآنِ فَلَا فَرْقَ بَيْنَ النَّظَرِ إِلَيْهِ وَبَيْنَ النَّظَرِ إِلَى رَسُولِ اللهِ **صَلَّى اللهُ عَلَيْهِ وَسَلَّمَ** فَكَأَنَّ القُرْآنَ أُنْشِأَ صُوْرَةً جَسَدِيَّةً يُقَالُ لَهَا مُحَمَّدٌ بْنُ عَبْدِ اللهِ بْنِ عَبْدِ المُطَّلِبِ **صَلَّى اللهُ عَلَيْهِ وَسَلَّمَ**.

Fa-man arāda an yarā Rasūlallāhi ***ṣallā Allāhu ʿalayhi wa sallama*** *mimman lam yudrikuhu min ummatihi fa-l-yanẓur ila-l-Qurʾāni fa-lā farqa bayna-n-naẓari ilayhi wa bayna-n-naẓari ilā Rasūlillāhi* ***ṣallā Allāhu ʿalayhi wa sallam*** *fa-kaʾanna-l-Qurʾāna unshiʾa ṣūratan jasadiyyatan yuqālu lahā Muḥammadun bin ʿAbdillāhi bin ʿAbdi-l-Muṭṭalibi* ***ṣallā Allāhu ʿalayhi wa sallam.***

Thus, whoever wants to see the Messenger of God ﷺ from among his community who did not live during his generation, let them look upon the Qurʾan, for there is no difference between gazing at it and the Messenger of God ﷺ. It is as if the Qurʾan was molded into a human form named Muhammad the son of ʿAbdullah the son of ʿAbd al-Muttalib ﷺ.

وَالقُرْآنُ كَلَامُ اللهِ وَهُوَ صِفَتُهُ فَكَانَ مُحَمَّدٌ صَلَّى اللهُ عَلَيْهِ وَسَلَّمَ صِفَةُ الحَقِّ تَعَالَى بِجُمْلَتِهِ فَمَنْ يُطِعْ الرَّسُولَ فَقَدْ أَطَاعَ اللهَ لِأَنَّهُ لَا يَنْطِقُ عَنْ الهَوَى فَهُوَ لِسَانُ حَقٍّ صَلَّى اللهُ عَلَيْهِ وَسَلَّمْ.

Wa-l-Qur'ānu Kalāmu-Llāhi wa huwa Ṣifatuhu fa-kāna Muḥammadun ***ṣallā Allāhu 'alayhi wa sallama*** *ṣifatu-l-Ḥaqqi Ta'āla bi-jumlatihi fa-man yuṭi'i-r-Rasūla fa-qad aṭā'a-Llāha li-annahu lā yanṭiqu 'ani-l-hawā fa-huwa lisānu ḥaqqin* ***ṣallā Allāhu 'alayhi wa sallam****.*

Moreover, the Qur'an is the Speech of God and His Attribute. Similarly, Muhammad ﷺ is the Attribute of the Real ﷻ in his entirety. Whoever obeys the Messenger ﷺ has obeyed God because he ﷺ does not speak from desire. Rather, he is a tongue of truth ﷺ.

وَصْلٌ فِي قَوْلِهِ تَعَالَى: ﴿بِسْمِ اللهِ الرَّحْمٰنِ الرَّحِيْمِ﴾

Waṣlun fī Qawlihi Ta'ālā: "Bismillāhi-r-Raḥmān-r-Raḥīm"

Regarding His Statement ﷻ: "In the Name of God, Most-Beneficent Most-Merciful"

فِي قَوْلِهِ "الرَّحِيمِ" مِنَ البَسْمَلَةِ الرَّحِيْمُ صِفَةُ مُحَمَّدٍ صَلَّى اللهُ عَلَيْهِ وَسَلَّمَ كَمَا قَالَ تَعَالَى ﴿بِالْمُؤْمِنِينَ رَؤُوفٌ رَحِيْمٌ﴾ (٩:١٢٨) وَبِهِ صَلَّى اللهُ عَلَيْهِ وَسَلَّمَ كَمَالُ الوُجُودِ وَبِالرَّحِيمِ تَمَّتْ البَسْمَلَةُ وَبِتَمَامِهَا تَمَّ العَالَمُ خَلْقًا وَإِبْدَاعًا فَالرَّحِيْمُ هُوَ مُحَمَّدٌ صَلَّى اللهُ عَلَيْهِ وَسَلَّمْ.

Fī qawlihi "Ar-Raḥīm" mina-l-Basmalati ar-Raḥīmu ṣifatu Muḥammadin ***ṣallā Allāhu 'alayhi wa sallam*** *ka-mā qāla Ta'ālā "bi-l-mu'minīna Ra'ūfun Raḥīm" wa bihi kamālu-l-wujūdi wa bi-r-Raḥīmi tammati-l-basmalatu wa bi-*

tamāmihā tamma-l-ʿālamu khalqan wa ibdāʿan fa-r-Raḥīmu huwa Muḥammadun ***ṣallā Allāhu ʿalayhi wa sallam****.*

Regarding His use of "Most-Merciful" in the *Opening*, this is the attribute of Muhammad ﷺ, just as God ﷻ has said: "With the believers, he is gentle and merciful". Also, through him ﷺ, existence was perfected just as through the Most-Merciful the *Opening* was completed. Thenceforth, through its completeness the world was also completed in creation and creativity. Thus, the merciful one is Muhammad ﷺ.

وَ "بِسْمِ" هُوَ أَبُونَا آدَمُ وَأَعْنِي فِي مَقَامِ ابْتِدَاءِ الأَمْرِ وَنِهَايَتِهِ وَذَلِكَ أَنَّ آدَمَ عَلَيْهِ السَّلَامُ هُوَ حَامِلُ الأَسْمَاءِ كَمَا قَالَ تَعَالَى ﴿وَعَلَّمَ آدَمَ الأَسْمَاءَ كُلَّهَا﴾ (٢:٣١) وَمُحَمَّدٌ **صَلَّى اللهُ عَلَيْهِ وَسَلَّمَ** حَامِلُ مَعَانِي تِلْكَ الأَسْمَاءَ الَّتِي حَمَلَهَا آدَمُ عَلَيْهِ السَّلَامُ وَهِيَ الكَلِمُ قَالَ **صَلَّى اللهُ عَلَيْهِ وَسَلَّمَ** "أُوْتِيتُ جَوَامِعَ الكَلِمِ" وَمَنْ أَثْنَى عَلَى نَفْسِهِ أَمْكَنُ وَأَتَمُّ مِمَّنْ أُثْنِيَ عَلَيْهِ كَيَحْيَى وَعِيسَى عَلَيْهِمَا السَّلَامْ.

Wa "B-ism" huwa abūnā Ādamu wa aʿnī fī maqāmi ibtidāʾi-l-amri wa nihāyatihi wa dhālika anna Ādama ʿalayhi-s-salāma huwa ḥāmilu-l-asmāʾi ka-mā qāla Taʿālā: "Wa ʿallama Ādama-l-Asmāʾa kullahā" wa Muḥammadun ***ṣallā Allāhu ʿalayhi wa sallama*** *ḥāmilu maʿānī tilka-l-asmāʾi allatī ḥamalahā kullahā Ādamu ʿalayhi-s-salāma wa hiya-l-kalimu. Qāla* ***ṣallā Allāhu ʿalayhi wa sallama*** *"Ūtītu Jawāmiʿa-l-Kalimi" wa man athnā ʿalā nafsihi amkanu wa attama mimman uthniya ʿalayhi ka-Yaḥyā wa ʿĪsā ʿalayhima-s-salām.*

As for "In the Name of", this is our father Adam ﷺ. This is

a reference to his station as the beginning of creation and its end. This is because Adam عليه السلام is the carrier of the Names, just as He ﷻ has said: "He taught Adam all the Names" (2:31). Meanwhile, Muhammad ﷺ is the carrier of the meanings of these Names which Adam carried in their entirety. These are the 'Divine Words'. He ﷺ said: "I was given the all-encompassing speech". The one who praises himself is more steadfast and perfect than they who are praised, such as John the Baptist and Jesus عليه السلام.

ثُمَّ وَجَدْنَا مِيمَ "بِسْمِ" الَّذِي هُوَ آدَمُ عَلَيْهِ السَّلَامُ مُعَرَّقًا وَوَجَدْنَا مِيمِ "الرَّحِيمِ" مُعَرَّقًا الَّذِي هُوَ مُحَمَّدٌ **صَلَّى اللهُ عَلَيْهِ وَسَلَّمَ** فَعَلِمْنَا أَنَّ مَادَّةَ مِيمِ آدَمَ عَلَيْهِ السَّلَامُ نَاتِجَةً عَنْ وُجُودِ عَالَمِ التَّرْكِيبِ إِذْ لَمْ يَكُنْ مَبْعُوثًا وَعَلِمْنَا أَنَّ مَادَّةَ مِيمِ مُحَمَّدٍ صَلَّى اللهُ عَلَيْهِ وَسَلَّمَ لِوُجُودِ الخِطَابِ عُمُومًا **صَلَّى اللهُ عَلَيْهِ وَسَلَّمْ**.

Thumma wajadnā mīma "B-ism" alladhī huwa Ādamu ʿalayhi-s-salāma muʿarraqan wa wajadnā mīma "ar-Raḥīm" muʿarraqan alladhī huwa Muḥammadun ***ṣallā Allāhu ʿalayhi wa sallama*** *fa-ʿalimnā anna māddata mīmi Ādama ʿalayhi-s-salāma nātijatan ʿan wujūdi ʿālami-t-tarkībi idh lam yakun mabʿūthan wa ʿalimnā anna māddata mīmi Muḥammadin* ***ṣallā Allāhu ʿalayhi wa sallam*** *li-wujūdi-l-khiṭābi ʿumūman* ***ṣallā Allāhu ʿalayhi wa sallam****.*
We also see that the letter *mīm* in "In the Name of", which is Adam عليه السلام has a long stem, just as the *mīm* of "Most-Merciful" also has a long stem, which is Muhammad ﷺ. In this way, we know that the material of this *mīm* of Adam عليه السلام emerges from the world of composition, since he was not sent as a messenger to anyone specifically. We also know

that the material of the *mīm* of Muhammad ﷺ is due to the universality of his address ﷺ humanity.

وَوَجَدْنَا فِي "بِسْمِ" الَّذِي هُوَ آدَمُ عَلَيْهِ السَّلَامُ أَلِفًا وَاحِدَةً خَفِيَتْ لِظُهُورِ البَاءِ وَوَجَدْنَا فِي "الرَّحِيمِ" الَّذِي هُوَ مُحَمَّدٍ **صَلَّى اللهُ عَلَيْهِ وَسَلَّمَ** أَلِفًا وَاحِدَةً ظَاهِرَةً وَهِيَ أَلِفُ العَلَمِ وَنَفْسُ سَيِّدِنَا مُحَمَّدٍ وَذَاتُهُ **صَلَّى اللهُ عَلَيْهِ وَسَلَّمَ**.

Wa wajadnā fī "B-ism" alladhī huwa Ādamu ʿalayhi-s-salāma alifan wāḥidatan khafiyat li-ẓuhūri-l-bāʾi wa wajadnā fī "ar-Raḥīm" alladhī huwa Muḥammadun ***ṣallā Allāhu ʿalayhi wa sallam*** *alifan wāḥidatan ẓāhiratan wa hiya alifu-l-ʿalami wa nafsu sayyidinā Muḥammadin wa dhātihi* ***ṣallā Allāhu ʿalayhi wa sallam.***

We also find in "In the Name of", which is Adam ﷺ, one *alif* which is hidden due to the appearance of the *bāʾ*. Meanwhile, we find in "Most-Merciful", Muhammad ﷺ, one *alif* that is apparent, which is the *alif* of definitions and Soul and Essence of our Master Muhammad ﷺ.

فَخَفِيَتْ فِي آدَمَ عَلَيْهِ السَّلَامُ الأَلِفُ لِأَنَّهُ لَمْ يَكُنْ مُرْسَلًا إِلَى أَحَدٍ فَلَمْ يَحْتَاجُ إِلَى ظُهُورِ الصِّفَةِ وَظَهَرَتْ فِي سَيِّدَنَا مُحَمَّدٍ **صَلَّى اللهُ عَلَيْهِ وَسَلَّمَ** لِكَوْنِهِ مُرْسَلًا فَطَلَبَ التَّأْيِيدَ فَأُعْطِيَ الأَلِفَ فَظَهَرَ بِهَا **صَلَّى اللهُ عَلَيْهِ وَسَلَّمْ**.

Fa-khafiyat fī Ādama ʿalayhi-s-salāma al-alifu li-annahu lam yakun mursalan ilā aḥadin fa-lam yaḥtāju ilā ẓuhūri-ṣ-ṣifati wa ẓaharat fī sayyidinā Muḥammadin ***ṣallā Allāhu ʿalayhi wa sallama*** *li-kawnihi mursalan fa-ṭalaba-t-taʾyīda* *fa u'tiya-l-alifu fa-ẓahara bihā* ***ṣallā Allāhu 'alayhi wa sallam.***

Thus, this *alif* was hidden in Adam ﷺ because he was not sent to anyone and, therefore, was not in need of this attribute to appear. On the other hand, it appeared in our Master Muhammad ﷺ because he was sent as a messenger, requested victory and was granted the *alif* through which he appeared in this world ﷺ.

وَوَجَدْنَا "بِسْمِ" ذَا نُقْطَةٍ وَ "الرَّحْمنُ" كَذَلِكَ وَ "الرَّحِيمُ" ذَا نُقْطَتَيْنِ وَاللهُ مُصْمَتٌ فَلَمْ تُوْجَدْ فِي اللهِ لَمَّا كَانَ الذَّاتُ وَوُجِدَتْ فِيمَا بَقِيَ لِكَوْنِهِمْ مَحَلَّ الصِّفَاتِ فَاتَّحَدَتْ فِي "بِسْمِ" آدَمَ لِكَوْنِهِ فَرْدًا غَيْرَ مُرْسَلٍ وَاتَّحَدَتْ فِي "الرَّحْمنَ" لِأَنَّهُ آدَمُ وَهُوَ الْمُسْتَوِي عَلَى عَرْشِ الكَائِنَاتِ الْمُرَكَّبَاتِ **صَلَّى اللهُ عَلَيْهِ وَسَلَّم.**

Wa wajadnā "B-ism" dhā nuqṭatin wa "ar-Raḥmān" kadhālika wa "al-Raḥīm" dhā nuqṭatayn wa-Llāhu muṣmatun fa-lam tūjad fi-Llāhi lammā kāna-dh-Dhātu wa wujidat fī-mā baqiya li-kawnihim maḥallu-ṣ-Ṣifāti fa-t-taḥadat fī "B-ism" Ādama li-kawnihi fardan ghayra mursalin wa-t-taḥadat fī "ar-Raḥmān" li-annahu Ādamu wa huwa-l-mustawī 'alā 'arshi-l-kā'ināti-l-murakkabāti ***ṣallā Allāhu 'alayhi wa sallam.***

We also see that "In the Name of" has one dot, "Most-Beneficent" as well, while "Most-Merciful" has two dots. Since God is a Mystery, His Name ﷻ did not include any dots, due to the power of the Divine Essence. Rather, it is found in everything else because they are subject to His Attributes. In this way, the two dots were united into one in "In the Name of", which is Adam ﷺ because he singularly was not sent as a messenger. The two dots also united in

"Most-Beneficent" because that also refers to Adam ﷺ who resides upon the throne of created and composite beings, ﷺ.

وَبَقِيَ الكَلَامُ عَلَى نُقْطَتَيْ "الرَّحِيمِ" مَعَ ظُهُورِ الأَلِفِ وَتَرْتِيبِ النُّقْطَتَيْنِ الوَاحِدَةَ مِمَّا تَلِي المِيمَ وَالثَّانِيَةِ مِمَّا تَلِي الأَلِفَ وَالمِيمَ فِي وُجُودِ العَالَمِ الَّذِي بُعِثَ إِلَيْهِمْ **صَلَّى اللهُ عَلَيْهِ وَسَلَّمَ** وَالنُّقْطَةُ الَّتِي تَلِيهِ أَبُو بَكْرٍ رَضِيَ اللهُ عَنْهُ.

Wa baqiya-l-kalāmu ʿalā nuqṭatiyyi "ar-Raḥīm" maʿa ẓuhūri-l-alifi wa tartībi-l-nuqṭatayni-l-wāḥidata mimmā tali-l-mīma wa-th-thāniyati mimmā tali-l-alifa wa-l-mīma fī wujūdī-l-ʿālami alladhī buʿitha ilayhim ***ṣallā Allāhu ʿalayhi wa sallama*** *wa-l-nuqṭatu allatī talīhi Abū Bakrin raḍiya Allāhu ʿanhu.*

What remains are the two dots in "Most-Merciful" alongside the apparent *alif* and arrangement of two dots, the first which follows the *mīm* and second which follows the *alif* and *mīm* in the existence of the world to which he (Muhammad) was sent, ﷺ. The dot that follows him ﷺ is Abu Bakr ؓ.

وَالنُّقْطَةُ الَّتِي تَلِي الأَلِفُ مُحَمَّدٌ **صَلَّى اللهُ عَلَيْهِ وَسَلَّمَ** وَقَدْ تَقَبَّبَتِ اليَاءُ عَلَيْهِمَا كَالغَارِ ﴿إِذْ يَقُولُ لِصَاحِبِهِ لَا تَحْزَنْ إِنَّ اللهَ مَعَنَا﴾ (٩:٤٠) فَإِنَّهُ وَاقِفٌ مَعَ صِدْقِهِ وَمُحَمَّدٌ **صَلَّى اللهُ عَلَيْهِ وَسَلَّمَ** وَاقِفٌ مَعَ الحَقِّ فِي الحَالِ الَّذِي هُوَ عَلَيْهِ فِي ذَلِكَ الوَقْتِ.

Wa-l-nuqṭatu allatī tali-l-alifu Muḥammadun ***ṣallā Allāhu ʿalayhi wa sallama*** *wa qad taqabbabati-l-yāʾu ʿalayhimā ka-l-ghāri idh yaqūlu li-ṣāḥibihi "lā taḥzan inna Allāha* *ma ʿanā" fa-innahu wāqifun maʿa ṣidqihi wa Muḥammadun* **ṣallā Allāhu ʿalayhi wa sallama** *wāqifun maʿa-l-Ḥaqqi fī-l-ḥāli alladhī huwa ʿalayhi fī dhālika-l-waqti.*

and the dot that follows the *alif* is Muhammad ﷺ. The *yāʾ* has also surrounded them like a cave, "Whence He told His Companion: 'Do not be sad, for surely God is with us!'" (9:40) Indeed, Abu Bakr ؓ is steadfast in his affirmation of the truth while Muhammad ﷺ is steadfast according to the specific manifestation at the time.

فَهُوَ الحَكِيْمُ صَلَّى اللهُ عَلَيْهِ وَسَلَّمَ كَفِعْلِهِ يَوْمَ بَدْرٍ فِي الدُّعَاءِ وَالإِلْحَاحِ وَأَبُو بَكْرٍ عَنْ ذَلِكَ صَاحٍ فَإِنَّ الحَكِيْمَ يُوْفِي المَوَاطِنَ حَقَّهَا وَلَمَّا لَمْ يَصِّحْ اجْتِمَاعُ صَادِقَيْنِ مَعًا لِذَلِكَ لَمْ يَقُمْ أَبُو بَكْرٍ فِي حَالِ النَّبِي صَلَّى اللهُ عَلَيْهِ وَسَلَّمَ وَثَبُتَ مَعَ صِدْقِهِ بِهِ.

Fa-huwa-l-ḥakīmu **ṣallā Allāhu ʿalayhi wa sallama** *ka-fiʿlihi yawma Badrin fī-l-duʿāʾi wa-l-ilḥāḥi wa Abū Bakrin ʿan dhālika ṣāḥin fa-inna-l-ḥakīma yūfī-l-mawāṭina ḥaqqahā wa lammā lam yaṣiḥḥ ijtimāʿu ṣādiqayni maʿan li-dhālika lam yaqum Abu Bakrin fī ḥāli-n-Nabiyyi* **ṣallā Allāhu ʿalayhi wa sallama** *wa thabata maʿa ṣidqihi bihi.*

Indeed, he is the wise ﷺ, as he did on the day of Badr when he insisted in his supplication while Abu Bakr ؓ was simply affirming the supplication. He who is wise fulfills duties according to circumstances. Since it is not fitting that two truthful ones be present at the same time, Abu Bakr ؓ did not stand in the state of the Prophet ﷺ. Rather, he remained in his truthfulness.

فَلَوْ فُقِدَ النَّبِيُّ صَلَّى اللهُ عَلَيْهِ وَسَلَّمَ فِي ذَلِكَ المَوْطِنِ وَحَضَرَهُ أَبُو

بَكْرٍ لَقَامَ فِي ذَلِكَ الْمَقَامِ الَّذِي أُقِيمَ فِيهِ رَسُولُ اللهِ **صَلَّى اللهُ عَلَيْهِ وَسَلَّمَ** لِأَنَّهُ لَيْسَ ثَمَّ أَعْلَى مِنْهُ يَحْجُبُهُ عَنْ ذَلِكَ فَهُوَ صَادِقُ ذَلِكَ الْوَقْتِ وَحَكِيمُهُ وَمَا سِوَاهُ تَحْتَ حُكْمِهِ **صَلَّى اللهُ عَلَيْهِ وَسَلَّمْ**.

Fa-law fuqida-n-Nabiyyi ***ṣallā Allāhu ʿalayhi wa sallama*** *fī dhālika-l-mawṭini wa ḥaḍarahu Abū Bakrin la-qāma fī dhālika-l-maqāmi alladhī uqīma fīhi Rasūlullāhi* ***ṣallā Allāhu ʿalayhi wa sallama*** *li-annahu laysa thamma aʿlā minhu yaḥjubuhu ʿan dhālika fa-huwa ṣādiqu dhālika-l-waqti wa ḥakīmuhu wa mā siwāhu taḥta ḥukmihi* ***ṣallā Allāhu ʿalayhi wa sallam****.*

If the Prophet ﷺ was missing from this event and Abu Bakr ؓ was present instead, then he would have established himself in that station of the Messenger of God ﷺ. This is because there is no one higher who can veil him ﷺ. He is the truthful and wise one and everyone is under his rule ﷺ.

وَصْلٌ فِي قَوْلِهِ تَعَالَى:

﴿مَثَلُ نُورِهِ كَمِشْكَاةٍ فِيهَا مِصْبَاحٌ﴾ (٢٤:٣٥)

Waṣlun fī Qawlihi Taʿālā: "Mathalu Nūrihi ka-Mishkātin fīhā Miṣbāḥun"

Regarding His Statement ﷻ: "His Light is like a Niche within which is a Lamp"

قَالَ تَعَالَى ﴿مَثَلُ نُورِهِ كَمِشْكَاةٍ فِيهَا مِصْبَاحٌ﴾ (٢٤:٣٥) فَشَبَّهَ نُورَهُ بِالْمِصْبَاحِ فَلَمْ يَكُنْ أَقْرَبُ إِلَيْهِ قَبُولًا فِي ذَلِكَ الْهَبَاءِ إِلَّا حَقِيقَةُ مُحَمَّدٍ **صَلَّى اللهُ عَلَيْهِ وَسَلَّمَ** الْمُسَمَّاةُ بِالْعَقْلِ فَكَانَ سَيِّدَ الْعَالَمِ **صَلَّى اللهُ عَلَيْهِ وَسَلَّمْ**.

Qāla Taʿālā: "Mathalu Nūrihi ka-Mishkātin fīhā Miṣbāḥun" fa-shabbaha nūrahu bi-l-miṣbāḥi fa-lam yakun aqrabu ilayhi qabūlan fī dhālika-l-habāʾi illā ḥaqīqatu Muḥammadin ***ṣallā Allāhu ʿalayhi wa sallama*** *al-musammāh bi-l-ʿaqli fa-kāna sayyida-l-ʿālami* ***ṣallā Allāhu ʿalayhi wa sallama****.*

He ﷻ said: "The example of His Light is like a Niche within which is a Lamp" (24:35) He compared His Light to a lamp. There is nothing in the *habāʾ* (primordial cloud) that has accepted this Light more than the reality of Muhammad ﷺ which is also known as the first intellect. This is why he is the master of existence ﷺ.

وَصْلٌ فِي قَوْلِهِ تَعَالَى:

﴿يَا أَيُّهَا النَّاسُ إِنَّا خَلَقْنَاكُمْ مِنْ ذَكَرٍ وَأُنْثَى﴾ (٤٩:١٣)

Waṣlun fī Qawlihi Taʿālā: "Yā ayyuhā-n-nāsu innā khalqnākum min dhakarin wa unthā"

Regarding His Statement ﷻ: "Oh people! Indeed, We have Created you from a male and female"

قَالَ تَعَالَى "يَا أَيُّهَا النَّاسُ إِنَّا خَلَقْنَاكُمْ" يُرِيْدُ آدَمَ عَلَيْهِ السَّلَامُ "مِنْ ذَكَرٍ" يُرِيْدُ حَوَّاءَ عَلَيْهَا السَّلَامُ "وَأُنْثَى" يُرِيْدُ عِيْسَى عَلَيْهِ السَّلَامُ وَمِنْ الْمَجْمُوعِ مِنْ ذَكَرٍ وَأُنْثَى يُرِيْدُ بَنِي آدَمَ بِطَرِيْقِ النِّكَاحِ وَالتَّوَالُدِ فَهذِهِ الآيَةُ مِنْ جَوَامِعِ الكَلِمِ وَفَصْلِ الخِطَابِ الَّذِي أُوْتِيهِ مُحَمَّدٌ صَلَّى اللهُ عَلَيْهِ وَسَلَّمْ.

Qāla Taʿālā: "Yā ayyuhā-n-nāsu innā khalaqnākum" yurīdu Ādama ʿalayhi-s-salāma "min dhakarin" yurīdu Ḥawwāʾa ʿalayha-s-salāma "wa unthā" yurīdu ʿĪsā ʿalayhi-s-salāma wa mina-l-majmūʿi min dhakarin wa unthā yurīdu banī Ādama bi-ṭarīqi-n-nikāḥi wa-l-tawāludi fa-hādhihi-l-āyatu min Jawāmiʿi-l-Kalimi wa faṣli-l-khiṭābi al-ladhī ūtīhi Muḥammadun ***ṣallā Allāhu ʿalayhi wa sallam.***

He ﷻ said: "Oh people! We have created you" meaning Adam ﷺ, "from a male" meaning Eve ﷺ "and female" meaning Jesus ﷺ. Then, the combination of male and female refers to the rest of sons of Adam through marriage and reproduction. This verse is included within the all-encompassing speech and definitive oration granted to Muhammad ﷺ.

وَصْلٌ فِي قَوْلِهِ تَعَالَى: ﴿وَأَلَّفَ بَيْنَ قُلُوبِهِمْ﴾ (٨:٦٣)

Waṣlun fī Qawlihi Taʿālā: "Wa allafa bayna qulūbihim"

Regarding His Statement ﷻ: "And He brought their hearts together"

مَنْزِلُ الأُلْفَةِ هُوَ مَنْزِلٌ وَاحِدٌ هَذَا مَنْزِلُ الأَعْرَاسِ وَالسُّرُوْرِ وَالأَفْرَاحِ وَهُوَ مِمَّا أُمْتَنَّ اللهُ بِهِ عَلَى نَبِيِّهِ مُحَمَّدٍ **صَلَّى اللهُ عَلَيْهِ وَسَلَّمَ** فَقَالَ ﴿لَوْ أَنْفَقْتَ مَا فِي الأَرْضِ جَمِيْعًا مَا أَلَّفْتَ بَيْنَ قُلُوبِهِمْ﴾ (٨:٦٣) يُرِيْدُ عَلَيْكَ "وَلَكِنَّ اللهَ أَلَّفَ بَيْنَهُمْ" يُرِيْدُ عَلَى مَوَدَّتِكَ وَإِجَابَتِكَ وَتَصْدِيْقِكَ **صَلَّى اللهُ عَلَيْهِ وَسَلَّمْ.**

Manzilu-l-Ulfati huwa manzilun wāḥidun hādhā manzilu-l-aʿrāsi wa-s-surūri wa-l-afrāḥi wa huwa mimmā imtanna Allāhu bihi ʿalā Nabiyyihi Muḥammadin ***ṣallā Allāhu ʿalayhi wa sallama*** *fa-qāla: "Law anfaqta mā fi-l-arḍi jamīʿan mā allafta bayna qulūbihim" yurīdu ʿalayka "Wa lākinna Allāha allafa baynahum" yurīdu ʿalā mawaddatika wa ijābatika wa taṣdīqika* ***ṣallā Allāhu ʿalayhi wa sallam.***
The abode of friendliness is a single abode. It is the station

of heavenly weddings, happiness and joys and is among what God has bestowed upon His Prophet Muhammad ﷺ when He said: "If you were to spend all what is on earth you would not bring their hearts together" (8:63), meaning upon you, "but God is the One Who brought them together", meaning towards your love, obedience and attesting to the truth of your message ﷺ.

اللّهُمَّ صَلِّ وَسَلِّمْ وَبَارِكْ عَلَيْهِ وَعَلَى آلِهْ

Allāhumma ṣalli wa sallim wa bārik ʿalayhi wa ʿalā ālih
Oh God, send your Prayers, Salutations and Blessings, upon Him and His Family.

بِسْمِ اللهِ الرَّحْمٰنِ الرَّحِيمِ

Bismillāhi-r-Raḥmāni-r-Raḥīm

In the Name of God, Most Beneficent Most Merciful

الفَصْلُ السَّادِس: حَقِيْقَةُ آل بَيْتِهِ ﷺ وَتَبْيِينُ مَقَامِهِمُ العَلِيِّ

Al-Faṣlu-s-Sādis: Ḥaqīqatu āli Baytihi ﷺ Wa Tabiyīnu Maqāmihimu-l-ʿAliyyi

Chapter Six: His Household ﷺ and Their Lofty Station

قَالَ رَسُولُ اللهِ **صَلَّى اللهُ عَلَيْهِ وَسَلَّمَ** "لِكُلِّ نَبِيٍّ آلٌ وَعُدَّةٌ وَآلِي وَعُدَّتِي الْمُؤْمِنُ" وَمِنْ أَسْمَائِهِ تَعَالَى الْمُؤْمِنُ وَهُوَ العُدَّةُ لِكُلِّ شِدَّةٍ وَالآلُ يُعَظِّمُ الأَشْخَاصَ فَعِظَمُ الشَّخْصِ فِي السَّرَابِ يُسَمَّى الآلَ فَآلُ مُحَمَّدٍ هُمُ العُظَمَاءُ بِمُحَمَّدٍ.

*Qāla Rasūlullāhi **ṣallā Allāhu ʿalayhi wa sallam**: "Li-kulli nabiyyin ālun wa ʿuddatun wa ālī wa ʿuddati-l-muʾmin" wa min Asmāʾihi Taʿālā al-Muʾmin wa huwa-l-ʿUdda li-kulli shidda wa-l-ʿālu yuʿaẓẓimu-l-ashkhāṣa fa-ʿiẓamu-sh-shakhṣi fi-s-sarābi yusamma-l-ālu fa-ālu Muḥammadin humu-l-ʿuẓamāʾu bi-Muḥammadin*

The Messenger of God ﷺ said: "For every prophet there is an *āl* [family] and sustenance. My *āl* and sustenance is *al-Muʾmin* [the believer]" Indeed, one of His Names ﷻ is *al-Muʾmin* [He who grants safety], because He is the sustenance for every difficulty. Also, the *āl* is what glorifies a person. This is why the greatness of a person that appears as a result of a mirage is called the *āl*. The family of Muhammad are those made great through Muhammad.

وَمُحَمَّدٌ صَلَّى اللهُ عَلَيْهِ وَسَلَّمَ مَثَلُ السَّرَابِ يَعْظُمُ مَنْ يَكُنْ فِيهِ وَأَنْتَ تَحْسَبُهُ مُحَمَّدًا صَلَّى اللهُ عَلَيْهِ وَسَلَّمَ العَظِيْمُ الشَّأْنِ كَمَا تَحْسَبُ السَّرَابَ مَاءً وَهُوَ مَاءٌ فِي رَأْيِ العَيْنِ فَإِذَا جِئْتَ مُحَمَّدًا صَلَّى اللهُ عَلَيْهِ وَسَلَّمَ لَمْ تَجِدْهُ، بَلْ وَجَدْتَ اللهَ فِي صُوْرَةٍ مُحَمَّدِيَّةٍ وَرَأَيْتَهُ بِرُؤْيَةٍ مُحَمَّدِيَّةٍ صَلَّى اللهُ عَلَيْهِ وَسَلَّمْ.

Wa Muḥammadun ***ṣallā Allāhu ʿalayhi wa sallama*** *mithla-s-sarābi yuʿaẓẓimu man yakūnu fīhi wa anta taḥsabuhu Muḥammadan* ***ṣallā Allāhu ʿalayhi wa sallama*** *al-ʿaẓīma-sh-shaʾni ka-mā taḥsabu-s-sarāba māʾan wa huwa māʾun fī raʾiyi-l-ʿayni fa-idhā jiʾta Muḥammadan* ***ṣallā Allāhu ʿalayhi wa sallama*** *lam tajidhu bal wajadta Allāha fī ṣūratin Muḥammadiyyatin wa raʾaytahu bi-ruʾyatin Muḥammadiyyatin* ***ṣallā Allāhu ʿalayhi wa sallam****.*

While he ﷺ is like the mirage, glorifying whoever resides within him, while you assume that such a person is Muhammad ﷺ of the lofty station, just as you assume the mirage is water, which it indeed is in the eye's opinion. Similarly, when you approach Muhammad ﷺ, you will not find him. Rather, you will find God in a Muhammadan form, which you perceive through a Muhammadan perception ﷺ.

كَمَا أَنَّكَ إِذَا جِئْتَ إِلَى السَّرَابِ لِتَجِدَهُ كَمَا أَعْطَاكَ النَّظَرُ فَلَمْ تَجِدْهُ فِي شَيْئِيَّتِهِ مَا أَعْطَاكَ النَّظَرُ، بَلْ وَجَدْتَ اللهَ عِنْدَهُ أَيْ عَرَفْتَ أَنَّ مَعْرِفَتَكَ بِاللهِ مِثْلَ مَعْرِفَتِكَ بِالسَّرَابِ أَنَّهُ مَاءً فَإِذَا بِهِ لَيْسَ مَاءً وَتَرَاهُ العَيْنُ مَاءً فَكَذَلِكَ إِذَا قُلْتَ عَرَفْتَ اللهَ وَتَحَقَّقْتَ بِالمَعْرِفَةِ عَرَفْتَ أَنَّكَ

مَا عَرَفْتَ اللهَ فَالعَجْزُ عَنْ مَعْرِفَتِهِ هِيَ المَعْرِفَةُ بِهِ **صَلَّى اللهُ عَلَيْهِ وَسَلَّمْ.**

*Ka-mā annaka idhā jiʾta ilā-s-sarābi li-tajidahu ka-mā aʿṭāka-n-naẓaru fa-lam tajidhu fī shayʾiyyatihi mā aʿṭāka-n-naẓaru bal wajadta-Llāha ʿindahu ay ʿarafta anna maʿrifatika bi-Llāhi mithla maʿrifatika bi-s-sarābi annahu māʾan fa-idhā bihi laysa māʾan wa tarāhu-l-ʿaynu māʾan fa-kadhālika idhā qulta ʿarafta-Llāha wa taḥaqqaqta bi-l-maʿrifati ʿarafta annaka mā ʿarafta Allāha fa-l-ʿajzu ʿan maʿrifatihi hiya-l-maʿrifatu bihi **ṣallā Allāhu ʿalayhi wa sallam**.*

When you reach the mirage to validate what your eyes have seen, you find it otherwise. You find God ﷻ there and come to know that your knowledge of Him is like that of the mirage and the extent to which it is water. It is not water, even though the eye sees it as such. Likewise, when you claim you know God and become certain of this, you come to know that you did not actually know Him ﷻ. Like so, our inability to know Him is knowledge of Him ﷺ.

فَمَا حَصَلَ بِيَدِكَ إِلَّا إِنَّهُ لَا يَتَحَصَّلُ لِأَحَدٍ مِنْ خَلْقِهِ وَكُلُّ مَنْ اسْتَنَدَ إِلَى اللهِ عَظُمَ فِي القُلُوبِ وَفِي العَارِفِينَ بِاللهِ وَعِنْدَ العَامَّةِ كَمَا أَنَّهُ مَنْ كَانَ فِي السَّرَابِ عَظُمَ شَخْصُهُ فِي رَأْيِ العَيْنِ وَيُسَمَّى ذَلِكَ الشَّخْصُ آلٌ وَهُوَ فِي نَفْسِهِ عَلَى خِلَافِ مَا تَرَاهُ العُيُونُ مِنْ التَّضَاؤُلِ تَحْتَ جَلَالِ اللهِ وَعَظَمَتِهِ كَذَلِكَ مُحَمَّدٌ **صَلَّى اللهُ عَلَيْهِ وَسَلَّمَ** يَتَضَاءَلُ تَضَاؤُلَ السَّرَابِ فِي جَنْبِ اللهِ لِوُجُودِ اللهِ عِنْدَهُ فَهَذَا إِذَا فَهِمْتَ مَا

قُلْنَاهُ مَعْنَى آلُ مُحَمَّدٍ صَلَّى اللهُ عَلَيْهِ وَسَلَّمْ.

Fa-mā ḥaṣala bi-yadayka illā annahu lā yataḥaṣṣalu li-aḥadin min khalqihi wa kullu mani-s-tanada illa-Llāhi ʿaẓuma fi-l-qulūbi wa fi-l-ʿārifīna bi-Llāhi wa ʿinda-l-ʿāmmati ka-mā annahu man kāna fi-s-sarābin ʿaẓuma shakhṣahu fī raʾyi-l-ʿayni wa yusammā dhālika-sh-shakhṣu ālun wa huwa fī nafsihi ʿalā khilāfi mā tarāhu-l-ʿuyūnu mina-t-taḍāʾuli taḥta Jalāli-Llāhi wa ʿAẓamatihi ka-dhālika Muḥammadun ***ṣallā Allāhu ʿalayhi wa sallama*** *yataḍāʾalu taḍāʾuli-s-sarābi fī Janbi-Llāhi li-Wujūdi Allāhi ʿindahu fa-hādhā idhā fahimta mā qulnāhu maʿnā Āli Muḥammadin* ***ṣallā Allāhu ʿalayhi wa sallam.***

What you realize is that it is not possible for any of His Creation to know Him ﷻ. Moreover, whoever is attributed to God becomes glorified in the hearts of both, the knowers of God and lay people, just as they appeared great in the mirage, according to the eye's gaze. This despite the fact that their reality is contrary to what the eyes perceive, due to their humility under the Majesty of God and His Greatness ﷻ. Like so is Muhammad ﷺ, he dwindles like the mirage in the presence of God since God is with him. If you understood what we have said, you will know the meaning of *Āl Muḥammad*.

وَلَمَّا كَانَ رَسُولُ اللهِ **صَلَّى اللهُ عَلَيْهِ وَسَلَّمَ** عَبْدًا مَحْضًا قَدْ طَهَّرَهُ اللهُ وَأَهْلَ بَيْتِهِ تَطْهِيرًا وَأَذْهَبَ عَنْهُمُ الرِّجْسَ وَهُوَ كُلُّ مَا يَشِينُهُمْ فَإِنَّ الرِّجْسَ هُوَ القَذَرُ عِنْدَ العَرَبِ قَالَ تَعَالَى ﴿إِنَّمَا يُرِيدُ اللهُ لِيُذْهِبَ عَنكُمُ الرِّجْسَ أَهْلَ البَيْتِ وَيُطَهِّرَكُمْ تَطْهِيرًا﴾ (٣٣:٣٣) فَلَا يُضَافُ إِلَيْهِمْ إِلَّا مُطَهَّرٌ وَلَا بُدَّ فَإِنَّ المُضَافُ إِلَيْهِمْ هُوَ الَّذِي يُشْبِهُهُمْ

فَمَا يُضِيفُونَ لِأَنْفُسِهِمْ إِلَّا مَنْ لَهُ حُكْمَ الطَّهَارَةِ وَالتَّقْدِيسِ.

Wa lammā kāna Rasūlullāhi ***ṣallā Allāhu ʿalayhi wa sallama*** *ʿabdan maḥḍan qad ṭahharahu Allāhu wa ahla baytihi taṭhīran wa adhhaba ʿanhumu-r-rijsa wa huwa kullu mā yashīnahum fa-inna-r-rijsa huwa-l-qadharu ʿinda-l-ʿArabi qāla Taʿālā: "Inna-mā yurīdu Allāhu li-yudhhiba ʿankumu-r-rijsa ahla-l-bayti wa yuṭahhirakum taṭhīra" fa-lā yuḍāfu ilayhim illā muṭahharun wa-lā budda fa-inna-l-muḍāfa ilayhim huwa al-ladhī yushbihuhum fa-mā yuḍīfuna li-anfusihim illā man lahu ḥukma-ṭ-ṭahārati wa-t-taqdīsi.*

And since the Messenger of God ﷺ is a pure and absolute servant, God has purified him and his family and pushed all filth away from them, meaning anything that disparages them. He ﷻ said: "Indeed, God wants to drive all filth away from you, oh people of the house and purify you immensely" (33:33). No one can be attributed to them save they who are purified. This is necessary because such a person resembles them. Thus, they only attribute to themselves whoever has obtained purity and holiness.

فَهَذِهِ شَهَادَةٌ مِنَ النَّبِيِّ **صَلَّى اللهُ عَلَيْهِ وَسَلَّمَ** لِسَلْمَانَ الفَارِسِيِّ بِالطَّهَارَةِ وَالحِفْظِ الإِلَهِي وَالعِصْمَةِ حَيْثُ قَالَ فِيهِ رَسُولُ اللهِ **صَلَّى اللهُ عَلَيْهِ وَسَلَّمَ** "سَلْمَانُ مِنَّا أَهْلُ البَيْتِ" وَشَهِدَ اللهُ لَهُمْ بِالتَّطْهِيرِ وَذَهَابِ الرِّجْسِ عَنْهُمْ **صَلَّى اللهُ وَسَلَّمَ عَلَيْهِ وَعَلَيْهِمْ أَجْمَعِينْ.**

Fa-hādhihi shahādatun mina-n-nabiyyi ***ṣallā Allāhu ʿalayhi wa sallama*** *li-Salmāna-l-Fārisiyyi bi-ṭ-ṭahārati wa-l-ḥifẓi-l-Ilāhiyyi wa-l-ʿIṣmati ḥaythu qāla fīhi Rasūlullāhi* ***ṣallā Allāhu ʿalayhi wa sallam****: "Salmānu minnā Ahlu-l-Bayt" wa shahida Allāhu lahum bi-t-taṭhīri wa dhahābi-r-rijsi ʿanhum* ***ṣallā Allāhu ʿalayhi wa ʿalayhim ajmaʿīn****.*

This is a testimony from the Messenger of God ﷺ for Salman the Persian of his purity and Divine Protection, whence the Messenger of God ﷺ said about him: "Salman is from us, the people of the house", just as God Attested for their purity and driving filth away from them ﷺ.

وَإِذَا كَانَ لَا يُضَافُ إِلَيْهِمْ إِلَّا مُطَهَّرٌ مُقَدَّسٌ وَحَصُلَتْ لَهُ العِنَايَةُ الإِلَهِيَّةِ بِمُجَرَّدِ الإِضَافَةِ فَمَا ظَنُّكَ بِأَهْلِ البَيْتِ فِي نُفُوسِهِمْ فَهُمْ المُطَهَّرُونَ بَلْ هُمْ عَيْنُ الطَّهَارَةِ **صَلَّى اللهُ وَسَلَّمَ عَلَيْهِ وَعَلَيْهِمْ أَجْمَعِينْ** فَهَذِهِ الآيَةُ تَدُلُّ عَلَى أَنَّ اللهَ قَدْ شَرَكَ أَهْلَ البَيْتِ مَعَ رَسُولِ اللهِ **صَلَّى اللهُ عَلَيْهِ وَسَلَّمَ** فِي قَوْلِهِ تَعَالَى ﴿لِيَغْفِرَ لَكَ اللهُ مَا تَقَدَّمَ مِنْ ذَنْبِكَ وَمَا تَأَخَّرَ﴾ (٢:٤٨).

Wa idhā kāna lā yuḍāfu ilayhim illā muṭahharun muqaddasun wa ḥaṣulat lahumu-l- ʿināyatu-l-ilāhiyyati bi-mujarradi-l-iḍāfati fa-mā ẓannuka bi-Ahli-l-Bayti fī nufūsihim fa-humu-l-muṭahharūna bal hum ʿaynu-ṭ-ṭahārati ***ṣallā Allāhu wa sallama ʿalayhi wa ʿalayhim ajmaʿīn*** *fa-hādhihi-l-āyatu tadullu ʿalā anna-Llāha qad ashraka Ahla-l-Bayti maʿa Rasūlillāhi* ***ṣallā Allāhu ʿalayhi wa sallama*** *fī qawlihi Taʿālā: "Li-yaghfira laka Allāhu mā taqaddama min dhanbika wa mā taʾakhkhara".*

Only a purified and holy one is attributed to them, who receive divine care simply because of this attribution. So, what do you suppose is the rank of the prophetic household? Indeed, they are the purified ones. Rather, they are the essence of purity ﷺ. This verse shows that God has admitted the prophetic household with the Messenger of God ﷺ as in His Statement: "So that God may forgive You what You have brought forth and what remains." (48:2).

فَطَهَّرَ اللهُ سُبْحَانَهُ نَبِيَّهُ صَلَّى اللهُ عَلَيْهِ وَسَلَّمَ بِالْمَغْفِرَةِ مَعَ أَنَّهُ لَمْ يَكُنْ لَهُ ذَنْبٌ فَدَخَلَ الشُّرَفَاءُ أَوْلَادُ فَاطِمَةَ كُلُّهُمْ وَمَنْ هُوَ مِنْ أَهْلِ الْبَيْتِ مِثْلُ سَلْمَانَ الْفَارِسِيِّ إِلَى يَوْمِ الْقِيَامَةِ فِي حُكْمِ هَذِهِ الْآيَةِ مِنَ الْغُفْرَانِ فَهُمُ الْمُطَهَّرُونَ اخْتِصَاصًا مِنَ اللهِ وَعِنَايَةً بِهِمْ لِشَرَفِ مُحَمَّدٍ وَعِنَايَةُ اللهِ بِهِ صَلَّى اللهُ عَلَيْهِ وَسَلَّمْ.

Fa-ṭ-ṭahhara Allāhu subḥānahu Nabiyyahu ***ṣallā Allāhu ʿalayhi wa sallama*** *bi-l-maghfirati maʿa annahu lam yakun lahu dhanbun fa-dakhala ash-shurafāʾu awlādu Fāṭimata kulluhum wa man huwa min Ahli-l-Bayti mithlu Salmāna-l-Fārisiyyu ilā Yawmi-l-Qiyāmati fī ḥukmi hādhihi-l-āyati mina-l-ghufrāni fa-humu-l-muṭahharūna ikhtiṣāṣan mina-Llāhi wa ʿināyatan bihim li-sharafi Muḥammadin wa ʿināyatu Allāh bihi* ***ṣallā Allāhu ʿalayhi wa sallam****.*

In this way, God ﷻ has purified His Prophet ﷺ with forgiveness even though he did not have any sins. Rather, this is to admit the noble ones, all the children of Fatima عليها السلام and whoever else is among the prophetic household like Salman the Persian until the Day of Judgment under the ruling of this verse. Indeed, they are the ones who are especially purified by God, due to Divine Care and the honor of Muhammad ﷺ.

فَأَرْجُو أَنْ يَكُونَ عَقِبَ عَلِيٍّ وَسَلْمَانَ تَلْحَقُهُمْ هَذِهِ الْعِنَايَةُ كَمَا لَحِقَتْ أَوْلَادَ الْحَسَنِ وَالْحُسَيْنِ وَعَقِبِهِمْ وَمَوَالِي أَهْلِ الْبَيْتِ فَإِنَّ رَحْمَةَ اللهِ وَاسِعَةٌ يَا وَلِيُّ صَلَّى اللهُ وَسَلَّمَ عَلَيْهِ وَعَلَيْهِمْ أَجْمَعِينْ.

Fa-arjū an yakūna ʿaqiba ʿAliyyin wa Salmāna talḥaquhum hādhihi-l-ʿināyatu ka-ma laḥiqat awlāda-l-Ḥasani wa-l-

Ḥusayni wa ʿaqibihim wa mawālī Ahli-l-Bayti fa-inna Raḥmata Allāhi Wāsiʿa yā Waliyyu ***ṣallā Allāhu wa sallam ʿalayhi wa ʿalayhim ajmaʿīn.***

Thus, I hope that the descendants of Ali and Salman ‎ؓ will also receive this Divine Care, just as it has reached the children of al-Hasan, al-Huseyn and their descendants along with the servants of the prophetic household. Indeed, the Mercy of God is vast oh saintly reader, ﷺ.

اللهُمَّ صَلِّ وَسَلِّمْ وَبَارِكْ عَلَيْهِ وَعَلَى آلِهْ

Allāhumma ṣalli wa sallim wa bārik ʿalayhi wa ʿalā ālih

Oh God, send your Prayers, Salutations and Blessings, upon Him and His Family.

بِسْمِ اللّٰهِ الرَّحْمٰنِ الرَّحِيْمِ

Bismillāhi-r-Raḥmāni-r-Raḥīm
In the Name of God, Most Beneficent Most Merciful

الفَصْلُ السَّابِعُ: فِي عُلُوِّ شَأْنِ شَرِيْعَتِهِ ﷺ وَنَسْخِهَا لِمَا قَبْلِهَا مِنَ الشَّرَائِعِ

Al-Faṣlu-s-Sābiʿ: Fī ʿUluwwi Shaʾni Sharīʿatihi ﷺ Wa Naskhihā li-mā qablihā mina-sh-Sharāʾiʿ

Chapter Seven: The Lofty Station of His Law ﷺ

فَكَانَ الحُكْمُ لَهُ بَاطِنًا أَوَّلًا فِي جَمِيْعِ مَا ظَهَرَ مِنْ الشَّرَائِعِ عَلَى أَيْدِي الأَنْبِيَاءِ وَالرُّسُلِ **عَلَيْهِمْ السَّلَامُ أَجْمَعِيْنْ** ثُمَّ صَارَ الحُكْمُ لَهُ ظَاهِرًا فَنَسَخَ كُلَّ شَرْعٍ أَبْرَزَهُ الإِسْمُ البَاطِنُ بِحُكْمِ الإِسْمِ الظَّاهِرِ لِبَيَانِ اخْتِلَافِ حُكْمِ الِاسْمَيْنِ.

Fa-kāna-l-Ḥukmu lahu bāṭinan awwalan fī jamīʿi mā ẓahara mina-sh-sharāʾiʾi ʿalā aydi-l-anbiyāʾi wa-r-rusuli ***ʿalayhimu-s-salamu ajmaʿīn*** *thumma ṣāra-l-ḥukmu lahu ẓāhiran fa-nasakha kulla sharʿin abrazahu-l-ismu-l-Bāṭinu bi-ḥukmi-l-ismi-ẓ-Ẓāhir li-bayāni-khtilāfi ḥukmi-l-ismayni.*

Indeed, the authority to rule was his ﷺ inwardly, at first, through all of what has appeared of Divine Laws on the hands of prophets and messengers عليهم السلام. Then, under the power of the Name 'The Outward', jurisdiction became his outwardly and abrogated every law which the Name 'The Inward' had brought forth, in order to clarify the difference between the two Names.

وَإِنْ كَانَ الْمُشَرِّعُ وَاحِدًا وَهُوَ صَاحِبُ الشَّرْعِ فَإِنَّهُ قَالَ كُنْتُ نَبِيًّا وَمَا قَالَ كُنْتُ إِنْسَانًا وَلَا كُنْتُ مَوْجُودًا وَلَيْسَتِ النُّبُوَّةُ إِلَّا بِالشَّرْعِ الْمُقَرَّرِ عَلَيْهِ مِنْ عِنْدِ اللهِ فَأَخْبَرَ أَنَّهُ صَاحِبُ النُّبُوَّةِ قَبْلَ وُجُودَ الأَنْبِيَاءِ الَّذِيْنَ هُمْ نُوَّابُهُ فِي هَذِهِ الدُّنْيَا **صَلَّى اللهُ عَلَيْهِ وَسَلَّمْ.**

Wa in kāna-l-musharriʿu waḥidan wa huwa ṣāḥibu-sh-Sharʿi fa-innahu qāla kuntu nabiyyan wa mā qāla kuntu insānan wa lā kuntu mawjūdan wa laysati-n-nubuwwatu illā bi-sh-sharʿi-l-muqarrari ʿalayhi min ʿindi-Llāhi fa-akhbara annahu ṣāḥibu-n-nubuwwati qabla wujūdī-l-anbiyāʾi al-ladhīna hum nuwwābuhu fī hādhihi-d-dunyā ***ʿalayhimu-s-salamu ajmaʿīn.***

This despite that the lawgiver is one: him ﷺ. He said: "I was a prophet" not "a human being" nor "physically existent." Prophethood can only be legislation from God ﷻ. He ﷺ informed us that he is the one granted prophethood before the existence of prophets who are in reality his deputies in this life ﷺ.

لَوْ كَانَ مُحَمَّدٌ **صَلَّى اللهُ عَلَيْهِ وَسَلَّمَ** قَدْ بُعِثَ فِي زَمَانِ آدَمَ لَكَانَتْ الأَنْبِيَاءُ وَجَمِيعُ النَّاسِ تَحْتَ حُكْمِ شَرِيْعَتِهِ إِلَى يَوْمِ القِيَامَةِ حِسًّا وَلِهَذَا لَمْ يُبْعَثْ عَامَّةً إِلَّا هُوَ خَاصَّةً فَهُوَ المَلِكُ وَالسَّيِّدُ وَكُلُّ رَسُولٍ سِوَاهُ فَبُعِثَ إِلَى قَوْمٍ مَخْصُوصِينَ.

Law kāna Muḥammadan ***ṣallā Allāhu ʿalayhi wa sallama*** *qad buʿitha fī zamāni Ādama la-kānati-l-anbiyāʾu wa jamīʿu-n-nāsi taḥta ḥukmi sharīʿatihi ilā yawmi-l-qiyāmati ḥissan wa li-hādha lam yubʿath ʿāmmatan illā huwa khāṣṣatan fa-huwa-l-maliku wa-s-sayyidu wa kullu rasūlin*

siwāhu fa-buʿitha ilā qawmin makhṣūṣīna.
Had Muhammad ﷺ been sent at the time of Adam عليه السلام, then all prophets and messengers would have been under his rule outwardly until the Day of Judgment. This is why no messenger had been sent generally except that he ﷺ is the one specified and addressed with that mission. He ﷺ is the king, master and every messenger other than him has only been sent to a specific people.

فَلَمْ تَعُمْ رِسَالَةُ أَحَدٍ مِنَ الرُّسُلِ سِوَى رِسَالَتُهُ **صَلَّى اللهُ عَلَيْهِ وَسَلَّمَ** فَمِنْ زَمَانِ آدَمَ عَلَيْهِ السَّلَامُ إِلَى زَمَانِ بَعْثِ مُحَمَّدٍ **صَلَّى اللهُ عَلَيْهِ وَسَلَّمَ** إِلَى يَوْمِ الْقِيَامَةِ مُلْكُهُ وَتَقَدُّمُهُ فِي الآخِرَةِ عَلَى جَمِيعِ الرُّسُلِ وَسِيَادَتُهُ فَمَنْصُوصٌ عَلَى ذَلِكَ فِي الصَّحِيحِ عَنْهُ.

Fa-lam taʿumma risālatu aḥadin mina-r-rusuli siwā risālatuhu ***ṣallā Allāhu ʿalayhi wa sallama*** *fa-min zamāni Ādama ʿalayhi-s-salāma ilā zamāni baʿthi Muḥammadin* ***ṣallā Allāhu ʿalayhi wa sallama*** *ilā yawmi-l-qiyāmati mulkuhu wa taquddumuhu fi-l-ākhirati ʿalā jamīʿi-r-rusuli wa siyādatahu fa-manṣūṣun ʿalā dhālika fi-ṣ-ṣaḥīḥi ʿanhu.*
No other message has encompassed all existent things except his message ﷺ. From the time of Adam عليه السلام until the time of Muhammad ﷺ and the Day of Judgment, all is his dominion. Moreover, his Superiority and mastery ﷺ above other messengers in the hereafter is clearly stated in the authentic narration.

فَرُوحَانِيَّتُهُ **صَلَّى اللهُ عَلَيْهِ وَسَلَّمَ** مَوْجُودَةٌ وَرُوحَانِيَّةُ كُلِّ نَبِيٍّ وَرَسُولٍ فَكَانَ الإِمْدَادُ يَأْتِي إِلَيْهِمْ مِنْ تِلْكَ الرُّوحِ الطَّاهِرَةِ بِمَا

يَظْهَرُونَ بِهِ مِنَ الشَّرَائِعِ وَالعُلُومِ فِي زَمَانِ وُجُودِهِمْ رُسُلًا **صَلَّى اللهُ عَلَيْهِ وَسَلَّمَ** لَكِنْ لَمَّا لَمْ يَتَقَدَّمْ فِي عَالَمِ الحِسِّ وُجُودِ عَيْنِهِ **صَلَّى اللهُ عَلَيْهِ وَسَلَّمَ** أَوَّلًا نُسِبَ كُلُّ شَرْعٍ إِلَى مَنْ بُعِثَ بِهِ وَهُوَ فِي الحَقِيْقَةِ شَرْعُ مُحَمَّدٍ **صَلَّى اللهُ عَلَيْهِ وَسَلَّمْ.**

fa-rūḥāniyyatahu ***ṣallā Allāhu ʿalayhi wa sallama*** *mawjūdatun wa rūḥāniyyatu kulli nabiyyin wa rasūlin fa-kāna-l-imdādu yaʾtī ilayhim min tilka-l-rūḥi-ṭ-ṭāhirati bi-mā yaẓharūna bihi mina-l-Sharāʾiʿ wa-l-ʿulūmi fī zamāni wujūdihim rusulan* ***ṣallā Allāhu ʿalayhi wa sallam*** *lākin lammā lam yataqaddam fī ʿālami-l-ḥissi wujūdu ʿaynihi* ***ṣallā Allāhu ʿalayhi wa sallama*** *awwalan nusiba kullu sharʿin ilā sharʿi man buʿitha bihi wa huwa fī-l-ḥaqīqati sharʿu Muḥammadin* ***ṣallā Allāhu ʿalayhi wa sallam****.*

His spirituality ﷺ is present while that of every prophet and messenger is receiving sustenance from this pure spirit, each according to what he brings of divine laws ﷺ. However, because his antecedence in creation was not present physically in this world, each law was attributed to the one with whom it was sent. In reality, they are all the law of Muhammad ﷺ.

فَلَا سَبِيْلُ أَنْ يَتَعَبَّدَ اللهَ أحداً بِشَرِيعَةٍ نَاسِخَةٍ لِهَذِهِ الشَّرِيعَةِ المُحَمَّدِيَّةِ وَإِنَّ عِيْسَى عَلَيْهِ السَّلَامُ إِذَا نَزَلَ مَا يَحْكُمُ إِلَّا بِشَرِيعَةِ مُحَمَّدٍ **صَلَّى اللهُ عَلَيْهِ وَسَلَّمَ** وَهُوَ خَاتَمُ الأَوْلِيَاءِ فَإِنَّهُ مِنْ شَرَفِ مُحَمَّدْ **صَلَّى اللهُ عَلَيْهِ وَسَلَّمَ** أَنْ خَتَمَ اللهُ وِلَايَةَ أُمَّتَهُ وَالوِلَايَةَ المُطْلَقَةَ بِنَبِيٍّ وَرَسُولٍ مُكْرَمْ فَلَهُ يَوْمَ القِيَامَةِ حَشْرَانِ يُحْشَرُ مَعَ الرُّسُلِ

رَسُولًا وَيُحْشَرُ مَعَنَا وَلِيًّا تَابِعًا مُحَمَّدًا صَلَّى اللهُ عَلَيْهِ وَسَلَّمْ.

*Fa-lā sabīlun an yataʿabbada Allāha aḥadun bi-sharīʿatin nāsikhatin li-hādhihi-sh-sharīʿati-l-muḥammadiyyati wa inna ʿĪsā ʿalayhi-s-salāma idhā nazala mā yaḥkumu illā bi-sharīʿati Muḥammadin **ṣallā Allāhu ʿalayhi wa sallama** wa huwa khātamu-l-awliyāʾi fa-innahu min sharafi Muḥammadin **ṣallā Allāhu ʿalayhi wa sallama** an khatama Allāhu wilāyata ummatihi wa-l-wilāyta-l-muṭlaqata bi-nabiyyin wa rasūlin fa-lahu yawma-l-qiyāmati ḥashrāni yuḥsharu maʿa-r-rusuli rasūlan wa yuḥsharu maʿanā waliyyan tābiʿan Muḥammadan **ṣallā Allāhu ʿalayhi wa sallam**.*

Thus, there is no path for anyone to worship God through a law that abrogates this Muhammadan law. When Jesus ﷵ descends he will not rule save through the Law of Muhammad ﷺ, and he will be the seal of saints. It is for the honor of Muhammad ﷺ that God has sealed the sainthood of his community and absolute sainthood with a noble prophet and messenger. This is why Jesus ﷵ will have two resurrections on the Day of Judgment: he will be sent forth with the messengers as one of them and with us as a saint and follower of Muhammad ﷺ.

اللهُمَّ صَلِّ وَسَلِّمْ وَبَارِكْ عَلَيْهِ وَعَلَى آلِهْ

Allāhumma ṣalli wa sallim wa bārik ʿalayhi wa ʿalā ālih

Oh God, send your Prayers, Salutations and Blessings, upon him and his family.

بِسْمِ اللَّهِ الرَّحْمَٰنِ الرَّحِيمِ

Bismillāhi-r-Raḥmāni-r-Raḥīm

In the Name of God, Most Beneficent Most Merciful

الفَصْلُ الثَّامِن: فِي اسْرَائِهِ وَمِعْرَاجِهِ ﷺ إِلَى حَضْرَةِ الحَقِّ عَزَّ وَجَلَّ

Al-Faṣlu-th-Thāmin: Fī ʿIsrāʾihi wa Miʿrājihi ﷺ *ilā Ḥaḍrati-l-Ḥaqqi* عَزَّ وَجَلَّ

Chapter Eight: His Ascension ﷺ

ثُمَّ إِنَّهُ لَمَّا وَصَلَ إِلَى المَقَامِ الَّذِي لَا يَتَعَدَّاهُ البُرَاقُ وَلَيْسَ فِي قُوَّتِهِ أَنْ يَتَعَدَّاهُ تَدَلَّى إِلَى الرَّسُولِ **صَلَّى اللهُ عَلَيْهِ وَسَلَّمَ** الرَّفْرَفُ فَنَزَلَ عَنْ البُرَاقِ وَاسْتَوَى عَلَى الرَفْرَفِ **صَلَّى اللهُ عَلَيْهِ وَسَلَّمْ.**

Thumma annahu lammā waṣala ilā-l-maqāmi alladhī lā yataʿaddāhu-l-burāqu wa laysa fī quwwatihi an yataʿaddāhu tadallā ila-r-Rasūli ***ṣallā Allāhu ʿalayhi wa sallama****-r-rafrafu fa-nazala ʿani-l-burāqi wa-s-stawā ʿala-r-rafrafi* ***ṣallā Allāhu ʿalayhi wa sallam.***

Then, when He reached the station which the heavenly steed cannot exceed and which is not in its power to exceed, the heavenly cushion descended to the Messenger ﷺ whence he descended from the steed and resided upon the heavenly cushion ﷺ.

صَعَدَ بِهِ الرَفْرَفُ وَفَارَقَهُ جِبْرِيْلُ فَسَأَلَهُ الصَّحَابَةُ فَقَالَ "أَنَّهُ لَا يَطِيْقُ

ذَلِكَ" وَقَالَ لَهُ "وَمَا مِنَّا إِلَّا لَهُ مَقَامٌ مَعْلُومٌ" فَلَوْ أَرَادَ الحَقُّ صُعُودَهُ فَوْقَ ذَلِكَ المَقَامِ لَكَانَ مَحْمُولًا مِثْلَ مَا حُمِلَ الرَّسُولُ **صَلَّى اللهُ عَلَيْهِ وَسَلَّمْ**.

Ṣaʿada bihi-r-rafrafu wa fāraqahu Jibrīlun fa-saʾalahu-ṣ-ṣaḥābatu fa-qāla annahu lā yuṭīqu dhālika wa qāla lahu: "Wa mā minnā illā lahu maqāmun maʿlūmun" fa-law arāda-l-Ḥaqqu ṣuʿūdahu fawqa dhālika-l-maqāmi la-kāna maḥmūlan mithla mā ḥumila-r-Rasūlu ***ṣallā Allāhu ʿalayhi wa sallam****.*

Then, the Heavenly Cushion ascended with him ﷺ and Gabriel ﷺ separated from him. When the Companions asked him ﷺ, he said: "He cannot withstand that" and Gabriel also said to him ﷺ: "There is none of us save that they have a known station" Indeed, if the Real ﷻ willed for him ﷺ to ascend above that station, he would have been carried like the Messenger ﷺ was also carried.

وَلَمَّا وَصَلَ المِعْرَاجُ الرَّفْرَفِيُّ بِالرَّسُولِ **صَلَّى اللهُ عَلَيْهِ وَسَلَّمَ** إِلَى مَقَامِهِ الَّذِي لَا يَتَعَدَّاهُ الرَفْرَفُ زُجَّ بِهِ فِي النُّورِ زَجَّةً غَمَرَهُ النُّورُ مِنْ جَمِيعِ نَوَاحِيْهِ وَأَخَذَهُ الحَالُ فَصَارَ يَتَمَايَلُ فِيْهِ تَمَايُلَ السِّرَاجِ إِذَا هَبَّ عَلَيْهِ نَسِيمٌ رَقِيْقٌ يُمِيلَهُ وَلَا يُطْفِئَهُ **صَلَّى اللهُ عَلَيْهِ وَسَلَّمْ**.

Wa lammā waṣala-l-miʿrāju-r-rafrafiyyu bi-r-Rasūli ***ṣallā Allāhu ʿalayhi wa sallama*** *ilā maqāmihi-l-ladhī lā yataʿaddāhu-r-rafrafu zujja bihi fi-n-nūri zajjatan ghamarahu-n-nūru min jamīʿi nawāḥīḥi wa akhadhahu-l-ḥālu fa-ṣāra yatamāyalu fīhi tamāyula-s-sirāji idhā habba ʿalayhi nasīmun raqīqun yumīluhu wa lā yuṭfiʾuhu* ***ṣallā Allāhu ʿalayhi wa sallam****.*

Then, when the ascension upon the heavenly cushion reached with the Messenger ﷺ a station after which it cannot proceed, he ﷺ was submerged within the Divine Light in such a way that it encompassed him ﷺ from all sides and he was overcome by such a spiritual state that he began to sway within the Light the way candlelight sways when it is overcome by a gentle breeze that does not extinguish it ﷺ.

وَلَمْ يَرَ مَعَهُ أَحَدًا يَأْنَسُ بِهِ وَلَا يَرْكَنُ إِلَيْهِ وَقَدْ أَعْطَتْهُ الْمَعْرِفَةُ أَنَّهُ لَا يَصِحُّ الْأُنْسُ إِلَّا بِالْمُنَاسِبِ وَلَا مُنَاسَبَةُ بَيْنَ اللهِ وَعَبْدِهِ وَإِذَا أُضِيفَتْ الْمُؤَانَسَةُ فَإِنَّمَا ذَلِكَ عَلَى وَجْهٍ خَاصٍّ يَرْجِعُ إِلَى الْكَوْنِ فَأَعْطَتْهُ **صَلَّى اللهُ عَلَيْهِ وَسَلَّمَ** هَذِهِ الْمَعْرِفَةُ الْوَحْشَةَ لِانْفِرَادِهِ بِنَفْسِهِ.

*Wa lam yara maʿahu aḥadun yaʾnasu bihi wa lā yarkan ilayhi wa qad aʿṭathu-l-maʿrifatu annahu lā yaṣiḥḥu-l-unsu illā bi-l-munāsibi wa lā munāsabatun bayna Allāhi wa ʿabdihi wa idhā uḍīfati-l-muʾānasatu fa-innamā dhālika ʿalā wajhin khāṣṣin yarjiʿu ilā-l-kawni fa-aʿṭathu **ṣallā Allāhu ʿalayhi wa sallama** hādhihi-l-maʿrifatu-l-waḥshata li-nfirādihi bi-nafsihi wa.*

There was no one with him ﷺ to keep him company or with whom he could speak. This is because he ﷺ knew, from the special knowledge given to him, that intimacy cannot occur save between likenesses, but there is none between God and His Servant. Even if intimacy were to occur, it would happen in a way that pertains to the universe. This knowledge is what caused him ﷺ to feel lonely, since he knew that he was alone in this journey.

وَهَذَا مِمَّا يَدُلُّكَ أَنَّ الإِسْرَاءَ كَانَ بِجِسْمِهِ **صَلَّى اللهُ عَلَيْهِ وَسَلَّمَ** لِأَنَّ

الأَرْوَاحَ لَا تَتَّصِفُ بِالوَحْشَةِ وَلَا الاسْتِيحَاشِ فَلَمَّا عَلِمَ اللهُ مِنْهُ ذَلِكَ وَكَيْفَ لَا يَعْلَمُهُ وَهُوَ الَّذِي خَلَقَهُ فِي نَفْسِهِ وَطَلَبَ **صَلَّى اللهُ عَلَيْهِ وَسَلَّمَ** الدُّنُوَّ بِقُوَّةِ المَقَامِ الَّذِي هُوَ فِيهِ فَنُودِيَ بِصَوْتٍ يَشْبَهُ صَوْتَ أَبِي بَكْرٍ تَأْنِيسًا لَهُ **صَلَّى اللهُ عَلَيْهِ وَسَلَّمْ.**

Hādhā mimmā yadulluka anna-l-isrāʾa kāna bi-jismihi ***ṣallā Allāhu ʿalayhi wa sallama*** *li-anna-l-arwāḥa lā tattaṣifu bi-l-waḥshahti wa-lā-l-istīḥāshi fa-lammā ʿalima Allāhu minhu dhālika wa kayfa lā yaʿlamahu wa Huwa-l-ladhī khalaqahu fī nafsihi wa ṭalaba* ***ṣallā Allāhu ʿalayhi wa sallama****-d-dunuwwa bi-quwwati-l-maqāmi-l-ladhī huwa fīhi fa-nūdiya bi-ṣawtin yushbihu ṣawta Abī Bakrin taʾnīsan lahu* ***ṣallā Allāhu ʿalayhi wa sallam.***

This is how you know that this ascension was in his body ﷺ because spirits cannot be attributed with loneliness. When God ﷻ knew this, and how can He not know when He created it in his soul ﷺ, the Messenger ﷺ requested company, through the power of that station, whence he was spoken to in a voice resembling that of Abu Bakr رضي الله عنه, to provide him ﷺ with intimacy.

اللهُمَّ صَلِّ وَسَلِّمْ وَبَارِكْ عَلَيْهِ وَعَلَى آلِهْ

Allāhumma ṣalli wa sallim wa bārik ʿalayhi wa ʿalā ālih

Oh God, send your Prayers, Salutations and Blessings, upon him and his family

بِسْمِ اللّٰهِ الرَّحْمٰنِ الرَّحِيمِ

Bismillāhi-r-Raḥmāni-r-Raḥīm

In the Name of God, Most Beneficent Most Merciful

الفَصْلُ التَّاسِع: فِي مَوْلِدِ حَقِيْقَتِهِ ﷺ قَبْلَ خَلْقِ الأَكْوَانِ وَظُهُوْرِ الأَعْيَانْ

Al-Faṣlu-t-Tāsiʿ: Fī Mawlidi Ḥaqīqatihi ﷺ *Qabla Khalqi-l-Akwāni wa Ẓuhūri-l-Aʿyān*

Chapter Nine: The Birth of His Reality ﷺ

اجْتَمَعَتْ الأَسْمَاءُ بِحَضْرَةِ المُسَمَّى اجْتِمَاعًا وِتْرِيًّا مُنَزَّهًا عَنْ العَدَدْ، فِي غَيْرِ مَادَّةٍ وَلَا أَمَدْ. فَلَمَّا أَخَذَ كُلُّ اسْمٍ فِيْهَا مَرْتَبَتَهُ وَلَمْ يَعُدْ مَنْزِلَتَهُ، فَتَنَازَعُوا الحَدِيْثَ دُوْنَ مُحَاوَرَةٍ وَأَشَارَ كُلُّ اسْمٍ إِلَى الَّذِي بِجَانِبِهِ دُوْنَ مُلَاصَقَةٍ وَلَا مُجَاوَرَةٍ.

Ijtimaʿati-l-Asmāʾu bi-ḥaḍrati-l-Musammā ijtimāʿan witriyan munazzahan ʿani-l-ʿadad, fī ghayri māddatin wa lā amad. Fa-lammā akhadha kullu ismin fīhā martabatahu wa lam yaʿid manzilatah, fa-tanāzaʿū-l-ḥadītha dūna muḥāwaratin wa ashāra kullu Ismin ila-l-ladhī bi-jānibihi dūna mulāṣaqatin wa-lā mujāwaratin.

The Divine Names gathered in the Presence of the Named, a singular meeting glorified above numbers, without physical matter or end. Each Name took its station and did not return to its abode. They conversed without speech. Each Name pointed to its Neighbor without adjacency.

وَقَالُوا: "يَا لَيْتَ شِعْرَنَا هَلْ يَتَضَمَّنُ الوُجُودُ غَيْرَنَا فَمَا عَرَفَ وَاحِدٌ مِنْهُمْ مَا يَكُونُ إِلَّا اسْمَانِ" أَحَدُهُمَا العِلْمُ المَكْنُونِ فَرَجَعَتْ الأَسْمَاءُ إِلَى الاسْمِ العَلِيمِ الفَاضِلْ.

Wa qālū: yā layta shiʿranā hal yataḍammanu-l-wujūdu ghayranā fa-mā ʿarafa wāḥidun minhum mā yakūnu "illā Ismāni" aḥaduhuma-l-ʿIlmu-l-Maknūnu fa-rajaʿati-l-Asmāʾu ila-l-Ismi-l-ʿAlīmi-l-Fāḍil.

They said: "We wish to know, does existence include other than Us?" None among them knew the answer except two Names, one of which is the Hidden Knowledge. Thus, all the Names returned to the Name 'The Knower' and Noble.

وَقَالُوْا: "أَنْتَ لَنَا الحَكَمُ العَادِلُ فَقَالَ: نَعَمْ بِسْمِ اللهِ وَأَشَارَ إِلَى الاسْمِ الجَامِعِ الرَّحمنِ، وَأَشَارَ إِلَى الاسْمِ التَّابعِ الرَّحِيمِ، وَأَشَارَ إِلَى الاسْمِ العَظِيمِ "وَصَلَّى اللهُ" وَرَجَعَ إِلَى الجَامِعِ مِنْ جِهَةِ الرَّحْمَةِ عَلَى النَّبِيِّ **صَلَّى اللهُ عَلَيْهِ وَسَلَّمَ.**

Wa Qālū: Anta lana-l-Ḥakamu-l-ʿĀdilu Fa-qāla: Naʿam Bismillāh wa ashāra ila-l-Ismi-l-Jāmiʿi-l-Raḥmān, wa ashāra ila-l-Ismi-l-Tābiʿi-r-Raḥīm, wa ashāra ila-l-Ismi-l-ʿAẓīmi: "wa ṣallā Allāhu" wa rajaʿa ila-l-Jāmiʿi min jihati-r-Raḥmati ʿala-n-Nabiyyi ***ṣallā Allāhu ʿalayhi wa sallama.***

They said: "You are our Just Judge!" He said: "Yes, In the Name of God, and pointed to the Encompassing Name the 'Most Merciful', then to the next Name, 'Most Beneficent', the 'Great' and [the Name:] 'Allah sent His Prayers', returning to the Encompassing Name from the side of Mercy upon the Prophet ﷺ.

وَأَشَارَ إِلَى الاسْمِ الخَبِيرِ، وَالعَلِيمُ مُحَمَّدٌ الكَرِيمُ **صَلَّى اللهُ عَلَيْهِ وَسَلَّمَ** وَأَشَارَ إِلَى الاسْمِ الحَمِيدِ، خَاتَمِ الأَنْبِيَاءِ **صَلَّى اللهُ عَلَيْهِ وَسَلَّمْ**، وَأَوَّلِ الأُمَّةِ وَصَاحِبِ لِوَاءِ الحَمْدِ وَالنِّعْمَةِ، فَنَظَرَ مِنَ الأَسْمَاءِ مَنْ لَمْ يَكُنْ لَهُ فِيمَا ذُكِرَ حَظٌّ، وَلَا جَرَى عَلَيْهِ مِنْ أَسْمَاءِ الكَرِيمِ لَفْظٌ.

Wa ashāra ila-l-Ismi-l-Khabīr, wa-l-ʿAlīm Muḥammadun al-Karīmu ***ṣallā Allāhu ʿalayhi wa sallama*** *wa ashāra ila-l-Ismi-l-Ḥamīd, Khātamu-l-Anbiyāʾi* ***ṣallā Allāhu ʿalayhi wa sallam****, wa awwalu-l-ummati wa ṣāḥibu liwāʾi-l-ḥamdi wa-l-niʿmati, fa-naẓara mina-l-Asmāʾi man lam yakun lahu fī-mā dhukira ḥaẓẓun, wa lā jarā ʿalayhi min Asmāʾi al-Karīmi lafẓun.*

He pointed to the Name 'The All-Aware' and the 'Knower', Muhammad the Generous ﷺ. Then, He pointed to the Name 'The One Who Deserves Praise', who is the Seal of Prophets ﷺ. The first of his community and wwner of the banner of praise and divine bounty ﷺ. Then, He ﷻ directed Himself towards Names that did not have a share in these mentions nor received an un utterance from the the Names of the Generous One.

وَقَالَ العَلِيمُ: مَنْ ذَا الَّذِي صَلَّيْتَ عَلَيْهِ، وَأَشَرْتَ فِي كَلَامِكَ إِلَيْهِ وَقَرَنْتَهُ بِحَضْرَةِ جَمْعِنَا، وَقَرَعْتَ بِهِ بَابَ سَمْعِنَا، ثُمَّ خَصَّصْتَ بَعْضَنَا بِالإِشَارَةِ وَالتَّقْيِيدِ إِلَى اسْمِهِ الرَّحِيمِ وَالحَمِيدِ، فَقَالَ لَهُ: يَا عَجَبًا وَهَذَا هُوَ الَّذِي سَأَلْتُمُونِي عَنْهُ أَنْ أُبَيِّنَهُ لَكُمْ تَحْقِيقًا، وَأُوَضِّحُ لَكُمْ إِلَى

مَعْرِفَتِهِ طَرِيقًا، هُوَ مَوْجُودٌ يُضَاهِيكُمْ فِي حَضْرَتِكُمْ.

Wa qāla al-ʿAlīmu: man dha-l-Ladhī ṣallayta ʿalayhi, wa asharta ilayhi fī Kalāmika ilayhi wa qarantahu bi-ḥaḍrati jamʿinā, wa qaraʿta bihi baba samʿinā, thumma khaṣṣaṣta baʿḍanā bi-l-ishārati wa-l-taqiyyīdi ilā ismihi-r-Raḥīmi wa-l-Ḥamīdi, fa-qāla lahu: yā ʿajaban wa hādhā huwa-l-ladhī saʾaltumūnī ʿanhu an ubayyinahu lakum taḥqīqan, wa uwaḍḍiḥu lakum ilā maʿrifatihi ṭarīqan, huwa mawjūdun yuḍāhīkum fī ḥaḍratikum.

The All-Knower said: "Who is this one upon whom You sent prayers and benedictions, pointed to in Your Speech, associated him in the Presence of Our Togetherness, knocked upon the door of Our Hearing through him then granted some of us the favor to point to his name including the Most-Beneficent and the one who deserves praise?" He ﷻ said to His Names: "How wondrous that you ask me about this one about whom I will inform You. He is a being whose rank rivals Your Presence.

وَظَهَرَ عَلَيْهِ آثَارُ نَفْحَتِكُمْ، فَلَا يَكُونُ فِي هَذِهِ الحَضْرَةِ شَيْءٌ إِلَّا وَيَكُونُ فِيهِ، وَيُحَصِّلَهُ وَيَسْتَوْفِيهِ، وَيُشَارِكَكُمْ فِي أَسْمَائِكُمْ، وَيَعْلَمُ بِهِ حَقَائِقَ أَنْبَائِكُمْ، وَعَنْ هَذَا المَوْجُودِ المَذْكُورِ، الصَّادِرِ مِنْ حَضْرَتِكُمْ. وَأَشَارَ إِلَى بَعْضِ الأَسْمَاءِ مِنهَا الوُجُودِ وَالنُّورِ، يَكُونُ هَذَا الوُجُودُ الكُنْهُ وَالكَيْفُ وَالأَيْنُ وَفِيهِ يَظْهَرُ بِالإِسْمِ الظَّاهِرِ حَقَائِقِكُمْ.

Wa ẓahara ʿalayhi āthāru nafḥatikum, fa-lā yakūnu fī hādhihi-l-ḥaḍrati shayʾun illā wa yakūnu fīhi, wa yuḥaṣṣilahu wa yastawfīhi, wa yushārikakum fī Asmāʾikum, wa yaʿlamu bihi ḥaqāʾiqa anbāʾikum, wa ʿan hādhā-l-mawjūdi-l-madhkūri, a-ṣ-ṣāḍiri min ḥaḍratikum, wa ashāra ilā baʿḍi-l-Asmāʾi minha-l-Wujūd wa-n-Nūr, yakūnu hādhā-l-wujūd al-kunhu wa-l-kayfu wa-l-aynu wa fīhi yaẓharu bi-l-Ismi-l-Ẓāhiri ḥaqāʾiqukum.

Yet the traces of your breezes appear upon him ﷺ. There is nothing in this presence except that exists through him and which he encompasses and gives due right. He also shares with you your names, and through these he knows the reality of Your News. Through this remembered existent being, who emanates from your presence – and He pointed to some Names like the Existence and Light – the entire universe will come to be, including the 'what', 'how' and 'where'. Through him ﷺ also appears the Name 'Outward' of your realities.

وَإِلَيْهِ بِالإِسْمِ المَنَّانِ وَأَصْحَابِهِ تَمْتَدُّ رَقَائِقُكُمْ **صَلَّى اللهُ عَلَيْهِ وَسَلَّمْ**، فَقَالُوْا أَنْبَهْتَنَا عَنْ أَمْرٍ، لَمْ نَكُنْ بِهِ عَلِيمًا وَكَانَ هَذَا الِاسْمُ إِشَارَتُهُ إِلَى المُتَفَضِّلِ عَلَيْنَا عَظِيمًا، فَمَتَى يَكُونُ هَذَا الأَمْرُ، وَيَلُوحُ هَذَا السِّرُّ؟

wa ilayhi bi-l-Ismi-l-Mannāni wa aṣḥābihi tamtaddu raqāʾiqukum ***ṣallā Allāhu ʿalayhi wa sallam****, fa-qālū anbahtanā ʿan amrin, lam nakun bihi ʿAlīman wa kāna hādha-l-Ismu ishāratuhu ila-l-Mutafaḍḍili ʿalaynā ʿaẓīman, fa-matā yakūnu hādhā-l-amru, wa yalūḥu hādha-s-sirru?*

Also, to him ﷺ through the Name the 'Bestower' and its Companions, your traces and subtleties will extend ﷺ." They said: "You have informed us of something about which we did not know. Indeed, this Name is an allusion to the one who has bestowed His Bounty upon us. So, when will this affair take place, and when will this secret be revealed?"

فَوَزَّعَتْ الأَسْمَاءُ كُلَّهَا مَمْلَكَةَ العَبْدِ الإِنْسَانِيِّ عَلَى هَذَا الحَدِّ الرَّبَّانِيِّ

وَتَفَاخَرَتْ فِي الحَضْرَةِ الإِلَهِيَّةِ الذَّاتِيَّةِ بِحَقَائِقِهَا وَبَيَّنَتْ حُكْمَ مَسَالِكِهَا وَطَرَائِقِهَا وَعَجِلُوا فِي وُجُودِ هَذَا الكَوْنِ رَغْبَةً فِي أَنْ يَظْهَرَ لَهُمْ عَيْنٌ، فَلَجَأُوا إِلَى الاِسْمِ المُرِيدِ المَوْقُوفِ عَلَيْهِ تَخْصِيصُ الوُجُودْ.

Fa-wazzaʿati-l-Asmāʾu kullahā mamlakata-l-ʿabdi-l-insāniyyi ʿalā hādhā-l-ḥaddi-l-rabbāniyyi wa tafākharat fi-l-Ḥaḍrati-l-Ilāhiyyati-dh-Dhātiyyah bi-ḥaqāʾiqihā wa bayyanat ḥukma masālikihā wa ṭarāʾiqihā wa ʿajilū fī wujūdi hādhā-l-kawni raghbatan fī an yaẓhara lahum ʿaynun, fa-lajaʾū ila-l-Ismi-l-Murīdi-l-mawqūfi fī takhṣīṣi-l-wujūd.

Then, all the Names spread forth the Kingdom of the Human Servant according to this Lordly Definition and showed pride in the Presence of the Divine Essence through their Realities and clarified the rulings of its paths. They insisted on the creation of this universe, out of desire to manifest Their Essences in this world. They sought refuge in the Name 'The One Who Wills', upon whom rests the task of bringing into existence.

وَقَالُوا: "سَأَلْنَاكَ بِهَذِهِ الحَضْرَةِ الَّتِي جَمَعَتْنَا وَتَحْقِيقِ الذَّاتِ الَّتِي شَمَلَتْنَا إِلَّا مَا عَلَّقْتَ نَفْسَكَ بِهَذَا الوُجُودِ المُنْتَظَرِ فَأَرَدْتَهُ، فَأَنْتَ يَا قَادِرٌ سَأَلْتُكَ بِذَلِكَ إِلَّا مَا أَوْجَدْتَهْ، وَأَنْتَ يَا حَكِيمٌ سَأَلْتُكَ بِذَلِكَ إِلَّا مَا أَحْكَمْتَهْ، وَأَنْتَ يَا رَحْمنُ إِلَّا مَا رَحِمْتَهُ **صَلَّى اللهُ عَلَيْهِ وَسَلَّمْ**، وَلَمْ تَزَلْ تَسْأَلْ كُلَّهَا وَاحِدًا وَاحِدًا قَائِمًا قَاعِدًا.

Wa qālū: saʾalnāka bi-hādhihi-l-ḥaḍrati-l-latī jamaʿatnā wa taḥqīqi-dh-dhāti-l-latī shamalatnā illā mā ʿallaqta Nafsaka bi-hādhā-l-wujūdi-l-muntaẓari fa-aradtah, fa-anta yā Qādirun saʾaltuka bi-dhālika illā mā awjadtah, wa anta yā Ḥakīmun saʾaltuka bi-dhālika illā mā aḥkamtah, wa anta yā Raḥmānu illā mā raḥimtah ***ṣallā Allāhu ʿalayhi wa sallam****, wa lam tazal tasʾal kullahā wāḥidan wāḥidan qāʾiman qāʿidan.*

They said: "We ask You by this Presence within which You have gathered us and the actualization of the Essence which has encompassed us, that You attach Yourself to this awaited being ﷺ and Will him into being. Indeed, You are the 'All-Powerful', we ask You through all of this to bring him into being. And You, Oh All-Wise, we ask You through all of this to grant him rule. And You, oh Most-Merciful, to bestow Mercy upon him ﷺ." In this way, each of them asked one by one, both standing and sitting.

فَعِنْدَمَا وَقَعَ هَذَا الكَلَامُ الأَنْفَسُ، فِي هَذَا الجَمْعُ الكَرِيمُ الأَقْدَسُ، تَعَطَّشَتْ الأَسْمَاءُ إِلَى ظُهُورِ آثَارِهَا فِي الوُجُودِ وَلَا سِيَّمَا الِاسْمِ المَعْبُودُ وَلِذَلِكَ خَلَقَهُمْ سُبْحَانَهُ وَتَعَالَى لِيَعْرِفُوهُ بِمَا عَرَفَهُمْ وَيَصِفُوهُ لِمَا وَصَفَهُمْ فَقَالَ:

Fa-ʿindamā waqaʿa hādhā-l-kalāmu-l-anfasu, fī hādhā-l-jamʿi-l-aqdas, taʿaṭṭashati-l-Asmāʾu ilā ẓuhūri āthārihā fi-l-wujūdi wa lā siyama-l-Ismu-l-Maʿbūdu wa li-dhālika khalaqahum Subḥānuhu wa Taʿālā li-yaʿrifūhu bi-mā ʿarafahum wa yaṣifūhu bi-mā waṣafahum fa-qāla:

When this most precious speech took place, in this most holy of gatherings, the Names became thirsty for their traces to appear in existence, most especially the Name: the Worshipped. This is why He ﷻ created creation, so that they know Him as He knows them, and attribute Him with what He attributed them with, whence He said:

﴿وَمَا خَلَقْتُ الْجِنَّ وَالإِنْسَ إِلَّا لِيَعْبُدُونِ مَا أُرِيدُ مِنْهُمْ مِنْ رِزْقٍ وَمَا أُرِيدُ أَنْ يُطْعِمُونِ﴾ (٥١:٥٦) فَلَجَأَتْ الأَسْمَاءُ كُلُّهَا إِلَى اسْمِ اللهِ الأَعَمِّ وَالرُّكْنِ القَوِيِّ الأَعْظَمِ.

"Wa mā khalaqtu-l-jinna wa-l-insa illā li-yaʿbudūni mā urīdu minhum min rizqin wa mā urīdu an yuṭʿimūni" fa-lajaʾati-l-Asmāʾu kulluhā ila-Ismi-Llāhi-l-Aʿammi wa-l-Rukni-l-Qawiyyi-l-Aʿẓami.

"I have not created the Jinn and mankind save to worship Me. I do not want from them any sustenance nor do I want them to feed Me" (51:56) Then, all the Names sought refuge in God's Universal Name and Strongest Pillar.

فَلَجَأَ الإِسْمُ الأَعْظَمُ إِلَى الذَّاتِ كَمَا لَجَأَتْ الأَسْمَاءُ وَالصِّفَاتُ، وَذَكَرَ الأَمْرَ وَأَخْبَرَ السِّرَّ فَأَجَابَ نَفْسَهُ المُتَكَلِّمُ بِنَفْسِهِ العَلِيمِ، إِنَّ ذَلِكَ قَدْ كَانَ بِالرَّحْمنِ فَقُلْ لِلإِسْمِ المُرِيدِ يَقُولُ لِلقَائِلِ بِأَمْرِ يَكُنْ، وَالقَادِرُ يَتَعَلَّقُ بِإِيجَادِ الأَعْيَانِ، فَيَظْهَرُ مَا تَمَنَّيْتُمْ، وَيَبْرُزُ لِعَيَانِكُمْ مَا اشْتَهَيْتُمْ.

Fa-lajaʾa-l-Ismu-l-Aʿẓamu ila-dh-Dhāti ka-mā lajaʾati-l-Asmāʾu wa-ṣ-Ṣifātu, wa dhakara-l-amra wa akhbara-s-sirra fa-ajāba Nafsahu-l-Mutakallima bi-Nafsihi-l-ʿAlīmi, inna dhālika qad kāna bi-r-Raḥmāni fa-qul li-l-Ismi-l-Murīdi yaqūlu li-l-Qāʾili yaʾmur yakun, wa-l-Qādiru yataʿallaqu bi-ījādi-l-aʿyāni, fa-yaẓharu mā tamannaytum, wa yabruzu li-aʿayānikum ma-shtahaytum.

The Greatest Name sought refuge in the Essence, as did the Names and Attributes. The Name mentioned the affair and uttered the secret. He addressed Himself the Speaker through His Self the Knower, that "Indeed this will come to be through the Most-Merciful. Thus, inform the Name 'The All-Aware' to tell the One who speaks 'Be!' And it will be!

And the 'All-Powerful' will fulfill the task of bringing the entities into being. In this way, what you have hoped for will appear, and what you have desired will emerge for You to witness."

فَتعَلَّقَتْ بِالإِرَادَةِ وَالعِلْمِ وَالقَوْلِ وَالقُدْرَةِ، (**سُبْحَانَ اللهِ وَالحَمْدُ للهِ وَلَا إِلَهَ إِلَّا اللهُ وَاللهُ أَكْبَر x4 وَلَا حَوْلَ وَلَا قُوَّةَ إِلَّا بِاللهِ العَلِيِّ العَظِيمِ فِي كُلِّ لَحْظَةٍ أَبَدًا عَدَدَ خَلْقِهِ وَرِضَا نَفْسِهِ وَزِنَةَ عَرْشِهِ وَمِدَادَ كَلِمَاتِهْ**) فَظَهَرَ أَصْلُ العَدَدِ وَالكَثْرَةِ وَذَلِكَ مِنْ حَضْرَةِ الرَّحْمَةِ، وَفَيْضِ النِّعْمَةِ، أَصْلُ الإِبْدَاءِ وَأَوَّلُ الإِنْشَاءِ نَشْأُ سَيِّدِنَا **مُحَمَّدٍ صَلَّى اللهُ عَلَيْهِ وَسَلَّمَ** عَلَى أَكْمَلِ وَجْهٍ وَأَبْدَعِ نِظَامٍ.

*Fa-ta'allaqat bi-l-Irādati wa-l-'Īlmi wa-l-Qawli wa-l-Qudrati, (***subḥānallah wa-l-ḥamdulillāh wa lā ilāha illā Allāh wa Allāhu Akbar x4 wa lā ḥawla wa lā quwatta illā billāhi-l-'Aliyyi-l-'Azīm fi kulli laḥzatin abadan 'adada khalqihi wa riḍā nafisihi wa zinata 'arshihi wa midāda kalimātih***) fa-ẓahara aṣlu-l-'adadi wa-l-kathrati wa dhālika min ḥaḍrati-r-Raḥmati, wa fayḍi-l-ni'mati, aṣlu-l-ibdā'i wa awwalu-l-inshā'i nash'u Sayyidinā Muḥammadin* ***ṣallā Allāhu 'alayhi wa sallama*** *'alā akmali wajhin wa abda'i niẓām.*

Divine Will became attached to His Knowledge, Speech and Power ﷻ. **(May Allah be Exalted, All Praise is due to Allah. There is no god but Allah, and Allah is the Greatest x4 There is no mean nor power save through Allah, the Loftiest and Greatest, in every moment, according to the number of His Creation, the Contentment of His Essence, the Weight of His Throne and Ink of His Words)** Then, the origin of numbers and multiplicity appeared from the Presence of Mercy and Flood of Divine Bounty. This original beginning and initial formation is that of our Master Muḥammad ﷺ.

صَلَّى اللهُ عَلَى مُحَمَّد، صَلَّى اللهُ عَلَيْهِ وَسَلَّمْ x3

Ṣallā Allāhu ʿalā Muḥammad ṣallā Allāhu ʿalayhi wa sallam

**May God send His prayers upon Muhammad,
May God send His prayers upon Him with peace.**

بِسْمِ اللّٰهِ الرَّحْمٰنِ الرَّحِيمِ

Bismillāhi-r-Raḥmāni-r-Raḥīm

In the Name of God, Most Beneficent Most Merciful

الفَصْلُ العَاشِر: مَحَلُّ القِيَامِ فِي حَضْرَةِ السَّلَام وَشُهُودِ بَدْرِ التَّمَام ﷺ

Al-Faṣlu-l-ʿĀshir: Maḥallu-l-Qiyāmi fī Ḥaḍrati-s-Salāmi wa Shuhūdi Badri-t-Tamām ﷺ

Chapter Ten: Standing in Sight of the Full Moon ﷺ

يَا نَبِي سَلَامْ عَلَيْكَ يَا رَوِي كَلَامَ الحَقِّ

يَا مَاحِي كُلَّ الذُّنُوبِ يَا ذِكْرَ الله نَفَحَاتُ الخَيْرِ أَنْتَ

Yā Nabī Salām ʿAlayka Yā Rawī Kalāma-l-Ḥaqqi
Yā Māḥī kulla-dh-Dhunūbi
Yā Dhikra Allāh
Nafaḥātu-l-Khayri Anta!

Oh Prophet, peace be upon you,
You who pours from Divine Speech
You, who erases all sins,
Oh, Remembrance of God
You are the breezes of goodness

ظَهَرَتْ أَنْوَارُ الحَقِّ كُشِفَتْ أَسْرَارُ القُدْسِ

أَشْرَقَ جَمَالُ الحَقِّ بِحَمْدِ الله تَجَلَّى فِي خَيْرِ عَبْدٍ

Ẓaharat anwāru-l-Ḥaqqi Kushifat asrāru-l-qudsi
Ashraqa Jamālu-l-Ḥaqqi
Bi-ḥamdi Allāh

Tajallā fī khayri 'Abdin
The Lights of the Real appeared,
The holy secrets are revealed
The Beauty of the Real has glowed,
Through God's Praise
It manifested in the Best of Servants

يَا نَبِي سَلَامٌ عَلَيْكَ يَا رَوِي كَلَامَ الحَقِّ
يَا مَاحِي كُلَّ الذُّنُوبِ يَا رُوحَ الله نَفَحَاتُ الخَيْرِ أَنْتَ

Yā Nabī Salām 'Alayka ***Yā Rawī Kalāma-l-Ḥaqqi***
Yā Māḥī kulla-dh-Dhunūbi
Yā Rūḥallāh
Nafaḥātu-l-Khayri Anta!
Oh Prophet, peace be upon you,
You who pours from Divine Speech
You, who erases all sins,
Oh, Spirit of God
You are the breezes of goodness

انْتَ يَا رُوحَ النُّبُوَّة انْتَ يَا ذَاتَ الوِلَايَة
انْتَ خَزَائِنُ الجُودِ يَا حَمْدَ الله وَفِيكَ بَابُ الوُصُولِ

Anta yā rūḥa-n-nubuwwa *Anta yā dhāta-l-wilāya*
Anta khazā'inu-l-jūdi
Yā Ḥamdallāh
Wa fīka bābu-l-wuṣūli
You, oh spirit of prophethood,
You, oh essence of sainthood
You are the treasuries of generosity,
Oh, Praise of God
In you is the gate of Divine Destination

يَا نَبِي سَلَامْ عَلَيْكَ   يَا رَوِي كَلَامَ الحَقِّ

يَا مَاحِي كُلَّ الذُّنُوبِ   يَا كَلِمَ الله   نَفَحَاتُ الخَيْرِ أَنْتَ

Yā Nabī Salām ʿAlayka ***Yā Rawī Kalāma-l-Ḥaqqi***
Yā Māḥī kulla-dh-Dhunūbi
Yā Kalimallāh
Nafaḥātu-l-Khayri Anta!

Oh Prophet, peace be upon you,
You who pours from Divine Speech
You, who erases all sins,
Oh, Words of God
You are the breezes of goodness

كَرُمَتْ بِكَ الأَخْلَاقُ   فَأَنْتَ يَدُ الخَلَّاقِ

وَانْطَوَتْ فِيْكَ الامْجَادُ   فِي حَمْدِ الله   وَأَنْتَ فَتْحُ الأَسْرَارِ

Karumat bika-l-akhlāqu *Fa-anta Yadu-l-Khallāqu*
Wa-nṭawat fīka-l-amjādu
Fī Ḥamdillāh
Wa anta fatḥu-l-asrāri

Through you manners are ennobled,
You are the Hand of the Divine Artist
Within you nobilities are enveloped
Within the Praise of God
Through you, secrets are opened

يَا نَبِي سَلَامْ عَلَيْكَ   يَا رَوِي كَلَامَ الحَقِّ

يَا مَاحِي كُلَّ الذُّنُوبِ   يَا سِرَّ الله   نَفَحَاتُ الخَيْرِ أَنْتَ

Yā Nabī Salām ʿAlayka ***Yā Rawī Kalāma-l-Ḥaqqi***
Yā Māḥī kulla-dh-Dhunūbi
Yā Sirrallāh
Nafaḥātu-l-Khayri Anta!

Oh Prophet, peace be upon you,
You who pours from Divine Speech
You, who erases all sins,
Oh, Secret of God
You are the breezes of goodness

نَسْأَلُكْ نَسْلَ البَتُولِ　　المَهْدِي قَلْبَ الرَّسُولِ

وَعِيْسَى ابْنَ البَتُولِ　　احْمَدَ الله　　فَهُمَا عَيْنُ القَبُولِ

Nas'aluk nasla-l-batūli *Al-Mahdī qalba-r-Rasūli*
Wa 'Īsā ibna-l-Batūli
Aḥmadallāh
Fa-humā 'ayna-l-qabūli

We seek from you the descendant of the chaste [Fatima],
The rightly guided ones and heart of the Messenger
And Jesus the son of the chaste [Mary]
Oh, the Highest Praise of God
For they both are the essence of acceptance

يَا نَبِي سَلَامْ عَلَيْكَ　　يَا رَوِي كَلَامَ الحَقِّ

يَا مَاحِي كُلَّ الذُّنُوبِ　　يَا حِبَّ الله　　نَفَحَاتُ الخَيْرِ أَنْتَ

Yā Nabī Salām 'Alayka ***Yā Rawī Kalāma-l-Ḥaqqi***
Yā Māḥī kulla-dh-Dhunūbi
Yā Ḥibballāh
Nafaḥātu-l-Khayri Anta!

Oh Prophet, peace be upon you,
You who pours from Divine Speech
You, who erases all sins,
Oh, Beloved of God
You are the breezes of goodness

مَرْحَبًا مَرْحَبًا يَا كُلَّ كُلِّي   مَرْحَبًا مَرْحَبًا لُبَّ الكَوْنَيْنِ

Marḥaban Marḥaban yā Kulla Kullī
Marḥaban Marḥaban Lubba-l-Kawnayni
Welcome welcome to the entirety of my entirety,
Welcome welcome to the heart of the two universes

مَرْحَبًا بِكَ أَنْتَ عَيْنُ الرَفْرَفْ   مَرْحَبًا يَا مَنْ قَابُ القَوْسِ فِيْكَ

Marḥaban bika anta ʿaynu-r-rafraf
Marḥaban ya man qābu-l-qawsi fīka
Welcome, you are the essence of the heavenly cushion
Welcome, the bow's length is within You

مَرْحَبًا مَرْحَبًا يَا كُلَّ كُلِّي   مَرْحَبًا مَرْحَبًا لُبَّ الكَوْنَيْنِ

Marḥaban Marḥaban yā Kulla Kullī
Marḥaban Marḥaban Lubba-l-Kawnayni
Welcome welcome to the entirety of my entirety,
Welcome welcome to the heart of the two universes

مَرْحَبًا وَرُوْحُكَ سِدْرُ العَرْشِ   مَرْحَبًا بِكَ يَا دُنُوِّ الأَدْنَى

Marḥaban wa rūhuka sidru-l-ʿarshi
Marḥaban bika yā dunuwwi-l-adnā
Welcome, your spirit is the lote tree of the throne,
Welcome, you who is the nearness beyond nearness

مَرْحَبًا مَرْحَبًا يَا كُلَّ كُلِّي   مَرْحَبًا مَرْحَبًا لُبَّ الكَوْنَيْنِ

Marḥaban Marḥaban yā Kulla Kullī
Marḥaban Marḥaban Lubba-l-Kawnayni
Welcome welcome to the entirety of my entirety,
Welcome welcome to the heart of the two universes

مَرْحَبًا بِمَنْ هُوَ بَحْرُ النُّورِ   مَرْحَبًا بِمَنْ هُوَ مَغزَى الوُجُودِ

Marḥaban bi-man huwa baḥru-n-nūri
Marḥaban bi-man huwa maghza-l-wujūdi
Welcome to he who is the ocean of light,
Welcome to he who is the meaning of existence

مَرْحَبًا مَرْحَبًا يَا كُلَّ كُلِّي   مَرْحَبًا مَرْحَبًا لُبَّ الكَوْنَيْنِ

Marḥaban Marḥaban yā Kulla Kullī
Marḥaban Marḥaban Lubba-l-Kawnayni
Welcome welcome to the entirety of my entirety,
Welcome welcome to the heart of the two universes

رَبِّ فَاكْشِفْ لِي سُتُورِي يَا الله   بِجَلِيلِ الشَانِ مُحَمَّد يَا الله

Rabbi fa-kshif lī sutūrī yā Allāh
Bi-jalīli-sh-shāni Muhammad yā Allāh
My Lord, lift my veils for me oh God,
By the lofty one Muhammad oh God

رَبِّ أَوْصِلْنَا إِلَيْهِ يَا الله   أَدْخِلْنَا فِي عَرْشِ قَلْبِهْ يَا الله

Rabbi awṣilnā ilayhi yā Allāh
Adkhilnā fī ʿarshi qalbih yā Allāh
My Lord, deliver us to him oh God,
Admit us to his heart's throne oh God

رَبِّ فَاكْشِفْ لِي سُتُورِي يَا الله   بِجَلِيلِ الشَانِ مُحَمَّد يَا الله

Rabbi fa-kshif lī sutūrī yā Allāh
Bi-jalīli-sh-shāni Muhammad yā Allāh
My Lord, lift my veils for me oh God,
By the lofty one Muhammad oh God

وَاجْعَلْنَا بِهِ وَفِيهِ يَا الله　　　　نَرَاهُ بِعَيْنِ أُوَيْسٍ يَا الله

Wa-j ʿalnā bihi wa fīhi yā Allāh
Narāhu bi- ʿayni Uwaysin yā Allāh
Make us through and within him oh God,
So that we see him with the eye of Uways oh God

رَبِّ فَاكْشِفْ لِي سُتُورِي يَا الله　　　　بِجَلِيلِ الشَّانِ مُحَمَّد يَا الله

Rabbi fa-kshif lī sutūrī yā Allāh
Bi-jalīli-sh-shāni Muhammad yā Allāh
My Lord, lift my veils for me oh God,
By the lofty one Muhammad oh God

حَتَّى نَرَاكَ بِذَاتِه يَا الله　　　　فِي عَيْنِ الكَمَالِ مُحَمَّدْ يَا الله

Ḥattā narāka bi dhatih yā Allāh
Fī ʿayni-l-kamāli Muḥammad yā Allāh
So that we see You through his essence, oh God,
In the essence of perfection Muhammad, oh God

رَبِّ فَاكْشِفْ لِي سُتُورِي يَا الله　　　　بِجَلِيلِ الشَّانِ مُحَمَّد يَا الله

Rabbi fa-kshif lī sutūrī yā Allāh
Bi-jalīli-sh-shāni Muhammad yā Allāh
My Lord, lift my veils for me oh God,
By the lofty one Muhammad oh God

صَلَّى اللهُ عَلَى مُحَمَّدْ صَلَّى اللهُ عَلَيْه وَسَلَّم x2

Ṣallā Allāhu ʿalā Muḥammad
Ṣallā Allāhu ʿalayhi wa sallam!
May God send His prayers upon Muhammad,
May God send prayers upon Him with peace

رَبِّ وَافْتَحْ قِبْلَتَيْنَا   عَيْنَ القَلْبِ وَالدُّعَاءِ

اَرِنَا بَدْرَ البُدُورِ   سِرَّ الكَوْنِ وَالوُجُودِ

Rabbi wa-ftaḥ qiblataynā *ʿAyna-l-qalbi wa duʿāʾi*
Arinā badra-l-budūri *Sirra-l-kawni wa-l-wujūdi*

Our Lord open our two directions,
The eye of the heart and supplication
Show us the fullest of all moons,
The secret of the universe and being

صَلَّى اللهُ عَلَى مُحَمَّدْ صَلَّى اللهُ عَلَيْه وَسَلَّم x2

Ṣallā Allāhu ʿalā Muḥammad
Ṣallā Allāhu ʿalayhi wa sallam!
May God send His prayers upon Muhammad,
May God send prayers upon Him with peace

تَكَرَّمْ عَلَى العِبَادِ   بِسِرِّ حُبِّ السِّرَاجِ

احْمَدَ كُلَّ الكَمَالِ   وَآلِهْ أَهْلَ الكِسَاءِ

Takarram ʿalā-l-ʿibādi *bi-sirri ḥubbi-s-sirāji*
Aḥmada kulla-l-kamāli *wa ālih ahla-l-kisāʾi*

Bestow upon Your Servants,
The secret of loving the serene lamp
Ahmad of all perfection,
And his family, the people of the mantle

صَلَّى اللهُ عَلَى مُحَمَّدْ صَلَّى اللهُ عَلَيْه وَسَلَّم x2

Ṣallā Allāhu ʿalā Muḥammad
Ṣallā Allāhu ʿalayhi wa sallam!
May God send His prayers upon Muhammad,
May God send prayers upon Him with peace

وَصَحْبِهِ أَهْلُ الوَجْدِ   وَمَنْ تَبعْ بِانْقِيَادِ

مِنْ إِمَامٍ ذِيْ وَرَعٍ   أَوْ كُلِّ فَانٍ بِسِرِّ

Wa ṣaḥbihi ahlu-l-wajdi   *Wa man tabiʿ bi-nqiyādi*
Min Imāmin dhī waraʿin   *Aw kulli fānin bi-sirri*

And his companions, the People of ecstasy,
And whoever followed them obediently
From every pious leader,
Or a saint annihilated in a Divine Secret

صَلَّى اللهُ عَلَى مُحَمَّدْ صَلَّى اللهُ عَلَيْه وَسَلَّم x2

Ṣallā Allāhu ʿalā Muḥammad
Ṣallā Allāhu ʿalayhi wa sallam!
May God send His prayers upon Muhammad,
May God send prayers upon Him with peace

يَا مُحيي الدِّينِ الأَكْبَرِ   صَاحِبُ خَتْمَ الفُتُوحِ

يَا سَيِّدِي بْنُ العَرَبِي   نَظْرَة لِقَلْبِ العَشُوقِ

Yā Muḥyi-d-Dīni-l-Akbari   *Ṣāḥibu Khatma-l-Futūḥi*
Ya sayyidi-bnu-l-ʿArabī   *Naẓra li-qalbi-l-ʿashūqi*

Oh, the greatest reviver of the religion,
Who is given the seal of openings
Oh, my master Ibn al-ʿArabi,
Gaze upon the heart of lovers

صَلَّى اللهُ عَلَى مُحَمَّدْ صَلَّى اللهُ عَلَيْه وَسَلَّم x2

Ṣallā Allāhu ʿalā Muḥammad
Ṣallā Allāhu ʿalayhi wa sallam!
May God send His prayers upon Muhammad,
May God send prayers upon Him with peace

وَيَا شَاهُ النَّقْشَبَنْدِي   تَكَرَّمْ يَا ذَا العَطَاءِ
عَبْدُ اللهِ الدَّاغِسْتَانِي   اجْعَلْنَا أَهْلَ الضِّيَاءِ

Wa yā Shāhu-n-Naqshabandī   Takarram yā dhā-l-ʿaṭāʾi
ʿAbdullāhi-d-Dāghestānī   Ijʿalnā ahla-ḍ-ḍiyāʾi

Oh, Shah al-Naqshabandi,
Show generosity oh generous one
Abdullah al-Daghestani,
Make us people of illumination

صَلَّى اللهُ عَلَى مُحَمَّدْ صَلَّى اللهُ عَلَيْهِ وَسَلَّم x2

Ṣallā Allāhu ʿalā Muḥammad
Ṣallā Allāhu ʿalayhi wa sallam!
May God send His prayers upon Muhammad,
May God send prayers upon Him with peace

يَا سُلْطَانَ الأَوْلِيَاءِ   شَيْخُنَا نَاظِمْ حَقَّانِي
افْتَحْ لَنَا ذِي العُيُونِ   لِتَرَاكُمْ فِي اللَّيَالِي

Yā ṣulṭāna-l-awliyāʾi   Shaykhunā Nāẓim Ḥaqqānī
Iftaḥ lanā dhī-l-ʿuyūnī   Li-tarākum fi-l-layālī
Oh, sultan of saints   Our guide Nazim Haqqani,
Open for us these eyes   to see you in dark nights

صَلَّى اللهُ عَلَى مُحَمَّدْ صَلَّى اللهُ عَلَيْهِ وَسَلَّم x2

Ṣallā Allāhu ʿalā Muḥammad
Ṣallā Allāhu ʿalayhi wa sallam!
May God send His prayers upon Muhammad,
May God send prayers upon Him with peace

يَا شَيْخُنَا القَبَّانِي   يَا مُتَصَرِّفَ الاقْطَابِ

يَا مَدَدَ الحَقِّ أَنْتَ غَوْثُنَا حَبْلَ الوُصُولِ

Yā shaykhunā al-Qabbānī *Yā mutaṣarrifa-l-aqṭābi*
Yā madada-l-Ḥaqqi anta *Ghawthunā ḥabla-l-wuṣūli*

Our Guide al-Kabbani,
Oh, Governor of Poles
Oh, sustenance given by the Real,
You are our salvation and rope to the destination

صَلَّى اللهُ عَلَى مُحَمَّدْ صَلَّى اللهُ عَلَيْهِ وَسَلَّم x2

Ṣallā Allāhu ʿalā Muḥammad
Ṣallā Allāhu ʿalayhi wa sallam!
May God send His prayers upon Muhammad,
May God send prayers upon Him with peace

آمِنَةْ أُمٌّ عَفِيفَةْ نَسْلُ أَحْمَدَ الشَّرِيفَةْ

بِنْتُهَا الحَجَّةْ نَزِيهَةْ مِنْ فَاطِمَةْ وَخَدِيجَةْ

Āminah ummun ʿafīfah *naslu Aḥmada-sh-sharīfah*
Bintuha-l-ḥajjah Nazīha *min Fāṭimah wa Khadījah*

Aminah is a chaste mother,
A noble descendant of Ahmad
Her daughter Hajjah Nazihah
From Fatimah and Khadijah

صَلَّى اللهُ عَلَى مُحَمَّدْ صَلَّى اللهُ عَلَيْهِ وَسَلَّم x2

Ṣallā Allāhu ʿalā Muḥammad
Ṣallā Allāhu ʿalayhi wa sallam!
May God send His prayers upon Muhammad,
May God send prayers upon Him with peace

يَا سَادَاتِي بِنْ عَلَوِي نَسْلُ المُهَاجِرْ عِيسَوِي

فَقِيهُنَا بِنْ عَلَوِي　　إِلَى عَيْنَاتِ بُو بَكْرِ

Ya sadātī bin 'Alawī　　Naslu-l-Muhājir 'Īsawī
Faqihūnā bin 'Alawī　　Ilā 'Aynāti bū Bakri

Oh, our masters the sons of 'Alawi,
Descendants of the migrant al-'Isawi
Our jurist the son of Alawi,
To the Aynat of Abu Bakr [B. Salim]

صَلَّى اللهُ عَلَى مُحَمَّدْ صَلَّى اللهُ عَلَيْهِ وَسَلَّم x2

Ṣallā Allāhu 'alā Muḥammad
Ṣallā Allāhu 'alayhi wa sallam!
May God send His prayers upon Muhammad,
May God send prayers upon Him with peace

وَالعَطَّاسُ آلُ الفَخْرِ　　كَذَا بِنْ شِهَابِ الحَمْدِ

وَلَا نَنْسَى ذَا الحَدَّادِ　　مَنْ بِهِ القُلُوبُ تَسْرِي

Wa-l- 'Aṭṭāsu ālu-l-fakhri　　Kadhā bin Shihabi-l-ḥamdi
Wa lā nansā dha-l-Ḥaddādi.　　Man bihi-l-qulūbu tasrī

And al-Attas, the family of exaltedness,
Likewise, the son of Shihab of praise
And we do not forget al-Haddad,
Through whom hearts can journey

صَلَّى اللهُ عَلَى مُحَمَّدْ صَلَّى اللهُ عَلَيْهِ وَسَلَّم x2

Ṣallā Allāhu 'alā Muḥammad
Ṣallā Allāhu 'alayhi wa sallam!
May God send His prayers upon Muhammad,
May God send prayers upon Him with peace

وَالسَّقَافُ أَهْلُ الوَصْلِ وَالمِحْضَارُ بَابُ الأُنْسِ

وَسُلْطَانُ العُلَمَاءِ سَالِمْ حَسَنْ وَبِنْ حَبْشِي

Wa-s-Saqqāfu ahlu-l-waṣli Wa-l-Miḥḍāru bābu-l-unsi
Wa ṣultānu-l-ʿulāmaʾi Sālim Ḥasan wa bin Ḥabshī

And al-Saqqaf the people of divine connection,
And Mihdar the door of Divine Intimacy
And the sultan of scholars
Salim, Hasan and sons of Habshi

صَلَّى اللهُ عَلَى مُحَمَّدْ صَلَّى اللهُ عَلَيْهِ وَسَلَّم x2

Ṣallā Allāhu ʿalā Muḥammad
Ṣallā Allāhu ʿalayhi wa sallam!
May God send His prayers upon Muhammad,
May God send prayers upon Him with peace

بِنْ حَفِيظْ خِتَامُ المِسْكِ أَهْلُ الوَرَعِ وَالرُّشْدِ

يَا نَسْلَ سَالِمَ السِّلْمِ وَلِي مُشْطَة وَذِي الوَادِي

Bin Ḥafīẓ khitāmu-l-miski Ahlu-l-wara'i wa-r-rushdi
Ya nasla Sālima-s-silmi Walī Mushṭa wa dhi-l-wādī

The sons of Hafidh, the seal of musk
The people of piety and maturity
Oh, descendants of the Salim of peace
The saint of Mushta and this entire valley [of Hadhramawt]

صَلَّى اللهُ عَلَى مُحَمَّدْ صَلَّى اللهُ عَلَيْهِ وَسَلَّم x2

Ṣallā Allāhu ʿalā Muḥammad
Ṣallā Allāhu ʿalayhi wa sallam!
May God send His prayers upon Muhammad,
May God send prayers upon Him with peace

مُحَمَّدْ أَهْلُ الشُّهُودِ   سَمَا ذِكْرًا ذِي الشَّهِيدِ
وَمِنْ عَلِي ذِي الْمَشْهُورِ   وَأَحْمَدْ عَطَاسُ الحِفْظِ

Muḥammad ahlu-sh-shuhūdi. Samā dhikran dhi-sh-shahīdi
Wa min ʿAliyyin dhi-l-Mashhūri Wa Aḥmad ʿAṭṭāsu-l-ḥifẓi
Muhammad [b. Salim] from the people of witnessing,
Of elevated mention is this martyr
And Ali the well-known,
And Ahmad Attas with protection

صَلَّى اللهُ عَلَى مُحَمَّدْ صَلَّى اللهُ عَلَيْهِ وَسَلَّم x2

Ṣallā Allāhu ʿalā Muḥammad
Ṣallā Allāhu ʿalayhi wa sallam!
May God send His prayers upon Muhammad,
May God send prayers upon Him with peace

جَوْهَرَةُ الْعُمْرِ عُمَرْ   شَيْخُنَا ابْنُ الْحَفِيظِ
مَظْهَرُ حَبِيبِ الْحَقِّ   لَامِعٌ فِي وَجْدِ الْقَلْبِ

Jawharatu-l-ʿumri ʿUmar   Shaykhunā ibnu-l-Ḥafīẓi
Maẓharu ḥabībi-l-Ḥaqqi   Lāmiʿun fī wajdi-l-qalbi
The jewel of our life Umar
Our guide, the son of Hafidh
The appearance of the Real's Beloved
Glowing in the heart's essence

صَلَّى اللهُ عَلَى مُحَمَّدْ صَلَّى اللهُ عَلَيْهِ وَسَلَّم x2

Ṣallā Allāhu ʿalā Muḥammad
Ṣallā Allāhu ʿalayhi wa sallam!
May God send His prayers upon Muhammad,
May God send prayers upon Him with peace

يَا سَائِرَ الأَوْلِيَاءِ   عَبْدُ القَادِرِ الجَيْلَانِي

يَا تِجَانِي مَعْ نِيَاسٍ   وَالشَّاذِلِي الرِّفَاعِي

Yā sā'ira-l-awliyā'i   *'Abdu-l-Qādir al-Jaylānī*
Yā Tijānī ma'-Niāsī   *Wa-sh-Shādhilī ar-Rifā'ī*
Oh, rest of saints   Abd al-Qadir al-Jaylani
Oh, Tijani with Niass   And al-Shadhili, al-Rifa'i

صَلَّى اللهُ عَلَى مُحَمَّدْ صَلَّى اللهُ عَلَيْهِ وَسَلَّمْ x2

Ṣallā Allāhu 'alā Muḥammad
Ṣallā Allāhu 'alayhi wa sallam!
May God send His prayers upon Muhammad,
May God send prayers upon Him with peace

يَا جَلَالُ الدِّينِ الرُّومِي   مَوْلَانَا حِبَّ الوَدُودِ

شَيْخُنَا بَيْرَامُ الصُّوفِي   يُونُسٌ فِي قَلْبِ الفَرْدِ

Ya Jalālu-d-Dīni-r-Rūmī   *Mawlānā ḥibba-l-Wadūdi*
Shaykhunā Bayrāmu-ṣ-ṣūfī   *Yūnusun fī qalbi-l-Fardi*
Oh, Jalal al-Din Rumi   Beloved of the Loving
Our guide Bayram the Sufi   Yunus is in His Heart

صَلَّى اللهُ عَلَى مُحَمَّدْ صَلَّى اللهُ عَلَيْهِ وَسَلَّمْ x2

Ṣallā Allāhu 'alā Muḥammad
Ṣallā Allāhu 'alayhi wa sallam!
May God send His prayers upon Muhammad,
May God send prayers upon Him with peace

كُلُّكُمْ أَحْمَدْ مُحَمَّدْ   يَا مَنْ بِهِ نَحْنُ نَحْمَدْ

فَالحَمْدُ مِنْكَ يَا رَبِّ   لِنِعْمَةِ خَيْرِ مُحَمَّدْ

Kullukum Aḥmad Muḥammad. Yā man bihi naḥnu naḥmad
Fa-l-Ḥamdu minka yā Rabbi Li-niʿmati khayri maḥmad

All of you are Ahmad Muhammad,
You, through whom we receive praise
Praise is from You, our Lord,
for the bounty of the best praise

صَلَّى اللهُ عَلَى مُحَمَّدْ صَلَّى اللهُ عَلَيْهِ وَسَلَّمْ x2

Ṣallā Allāhu ʿalā Muḥammad
Ṣallā Allāhu ʿalayhi wa sallam!
May God send His prayers upon Muhammad,
May God send prayers upon Him with peace

اللهُمَّ صَلِّ وَسَلِّمْ وَبَارِكْ عَلَيْهِ وَعَلَى آلِهْ

Allāhumma ṣalli wa sallim wa bārik ʿalayhi wa ʿalā ālih
Oh God, send your Prayers, Salutations and Blessings, upon him and his Family

بِسْمِ اللَّهِ الرَّحْمَٰنِ الرَّحِيمِ

Bismillāhi-r-Raḥmāni-r-Raḥīm
In the Name of God, Most Beneficent Most Merciful

الفَصْلُ الحَادِي عَشَر:
دُعَاءُ مِسْكِ الخِتَامِ مِنْ كَلَامِ الشَّيْخِ الأَكْبَرِ خَتْمِ الأَعْلَامِ المُسَمَّى بِالصَّلَاةِ الفَيْضِيَّةِ عَلَى حَبِيبِ الرَّبِّ العَلَّامِ ﷺ

Al-Faṣlu-l-Ḥādī ʿAshar: Duʿāʾu Miski-l-Khitāmi min Kalāmi-sh-Shaykhi-l-Akbari Khatmi-l-Aʿlāmi-l-Musammā bi-ṣ-Ṣalāti-l-Fayḍayyati ʿalā Ḥabībi-r-Rabbi-l-ʿAllām ﷺ

Chapter Eleven: Benedictions Upon the Beloved ﷺ

اللَّهُمَّ أَفِضْ صِلَةَ صَلَوَاتِكَ وَسَلَامَةَ تَسْلِيمَاتِكَ

Allāhumma afiḍ ṣilata ṣalawātika wa salāmata taslīmātika
Oh God, unfold the Intimacy of Your Prayers and Peace of Your Salutations

عَلَى أَوَّلِ التَّعَيُّنَاتِ المُفَاضَةِ مِنَ العَمَاءِ الرَّبَّانِي

ʿalā awwali-t-taʿayyunāti-l-mufāḍati mina-l-ʿamāʾi-r-Rabbānī
Upon the first of entities overflowing from the Lordly Cloud

وَآخِرِ التَّنَزُّلَاتِ المُضَافَةِ إِلَى النَّوْعِ الإِنْسَانِي

wa ākhiri-t-tanazzulāti-l-muḍāfati ilā-n-nawʿ il-insānī
And he who is the final descent to the human species

الْمُهَاجِرِ مِنْ مَكَّةَ "كَانَ اللهُ وَلَمْ يَكُنْ مَعَهُ شَيْءٌ ثَانٍ"

al-muhājiri min Makkata
"Kāna Allāhu wa lam yakun maʿahu shayʾun thānin"
He who migrates from the Mecca of
"God was and no second thing was with Him"

إِلى مَدِينَةِ "وَهُوَ الآنَ عَلَى مَا عَلَيْهِ كَانْ"

ilā Madīnati "Wa huwa-l-āna ʿalā mā ʿalayhi kān"
To the Madina of "And He is now as He has always been"

مُحْصِي عَوَالِمَ الحَضَرَاتِ الإِلَهِيَّةِ الخَمْسِ فِي وُجُودِهِ "وَكُلَّ شَيْءٍ أَحْصَيْنَاهُ فِي إِمَامٍ مُبِينْ"

Muḥsī ʿawālima-l-ḥaḍarāti-l-ilāhiyyati-l-khamsi fī wujūdihi
"Wa kulla shayʾin aḥṣaynāhu fī imāmin mubīn"
The gatherer of the Five Divine Presences in his being:
"And everything We have gathered in an evident leader"

وَرَاحِمِ سَائِلِي اسْتِعْدَادَاتِهَا بِنِدَاءِ جُودِهِ "وَمَا أَرْسَلْنَاكَ إِلَّا رَحْمَةً لِلْعَالَمِينَ"

wa rāḥimi sāʾilī istiʿdādātihā bi-nidāʾi jūdihi
"Wa mā arsalnāka illā raḥmatan li-l- ʿālamīn"
He who shows mercy towards dispositions, in generosity:
"We have not sent you but as a mercy to the worlds"

نُقْطَةِ البَسْمَلَةِ الجَامِعَةِ لِمَا يَكُونُ وَلِمَا كَانْ

nuqṭati-l-basmalati-l-jāmiʿati li-mā yakūnu wa li-mā kān
The dot of Opening, encompassing what was and will be

وَنُقْطَةِ الأَمْرِ الجَوَّالَةِ بِدَوَائِرِ الأَكْوَانْ

wa nuqṭati-l-amri-l-jawwālati bi-dawāʾiri-l-akwān
The dot of command, encircling the cosmic cycles

سِرِّ الهُوِيَّةِ التِي فِي كُلِّ شَيْءٍ سَارِيَةٌ

sirri-l-huwiyyati-l-latī fī kulli shayʾin sāriyatun
The secret of the Divine Essence, permeating all things

وَعَنْ كُلِّ شَيْءٍ مُجَرَّدَةٌ وَعَارِيَةٌ

wa ʿan kulli shayʾin mujarradatun wa ʿāriyatun
Yet, from all things abstracted and independent

أَمِينِ اَللهِ عَلَى خَزَائِنِ الفَوَاضِلِ وَمُسْتَوْدَعِهَا

amīni Allāhi ʿalā khazāʾini-l-fawāḍili wa mustawdaʿihā
God's trustee upon His treasuries, and their vessel

وَمُقَسِّمُهَا عَلَى حَسَبِ القَوَابِلِ وَمُوَزِّعُهَا

wa muqassimuhā ʿalā ḥasabi-l-qawābili wa muwazziʿuhā
And their dispenser according to different molds

كَلِمَةِ الإِسْمِ الأَعْظَمْ وَفَاتِحَةِ الكَنْزِ المُطَلْسَمْ

kalimati-l-ismi-l-Aʿẓam wa fātiḥati-l-kanzi-l-muṭalsam
The word of the Greatest Name and opening of the concealed treasure

المَظْهَرْ الأَتَمِّ الجَامِعِ بَيْنَ العُبُودِيَّةِ وَالرُّبُوبِيَّةِ

al-maẓhar al-atammi-l-jāmiʿi bayna-l-ʿubūdiyyah wa-r-rubūbiyyah

The complete appearance combining servanthood and lordship

وَالنَّشْأَةِ الأَعَمِّ الشَّامِلِ لِلإِمْكَانِيَّةِ وَالوُجُوبِيَّةِ

wa-n-nashʾati-l-aʿammi-sh-shāmili li-l-imkāniyyah wa-l-wujūbiyyah

The universal form, encompassing possibility and necessity

الطَّوْدِ الأَشَمِّ الَّذِي لَمْ يُزَحْزِحْهُ تَجَلِّي التَعَيُّنَاتِ عَنْ مَقَامِ التَمَكُّنِ وَالتَمْكِينْ

a-ṭ-ṭawdi-l-ashammi al-ladhī lam yuzaḥziḥhu tajalli-t-taʿayyunāt ʿan maqāmi-t-tamakkuni wa-t-tamkīn

The lofty mountain, unshaken by the manifesting entities from the firm station

وَالبَحْرِ الخِضَمْ الَّذِي لَمْ تُعَكِّرْهُ جِيَفِ الغَفَلَاتِ عَنْ صَفَاءِ اليَقِينْ

wa-l-baḥri-l-khiḍam al-ladhī lam tuʿakkirhu jiyafi-l-ghafalāti ʿan ṣafāʾi-l-yaqīn

The overflowing sea, undistracted from the purity of certainty by the filth of heedlessness

القَلَمِ النُّورَانِيِّ الجَارِي بِمِدَادِ الحُرُوفِ العَالِيَاتْ

al-qalami-n-nūrāniyyi-l-jārī bi-midādi-l-ḥurūfi-l-ʿāliyāt

The luminous pen moving through the ink of lofty letters

وَالنَّفَسِ الرَّحْمَانِي السَّارِي بِمَوَادِ الكَلِمَاتِ التَّامَّاتْ

wa-n-nafasi-r-raḥmānī as-sārī bi-mawādi-l-kalimāti-t-tāmmāt

The merciful breath permeating the completed words

الفَيْضِ الأَقْدَسِ الذَّاتِي الَّذِي تَعَيَّنَتْ بِهِ الأَعْيَانُ وَاسْتِعْدَادَاتُهَا

al-fayḍi-l-aqdasi-dh-dhātī al-ladhī taʿayyanat bihi-l-aʿyānu wa-stiʿdādātuhā
The holiest manifestation of the Divine Essence, through which entities and their dispositions were designated

وَالفَيْضِ المُقَدَّسِ الصِّفَاتِي الَّذِي تَكَوَّنَتْ بِهِ الأَكْوَانُ وَاسْتِمْدَادَاتُهَا

wa-l-fayḍi-l-muqaddasi-ṣ-ṣifātī al-ladhī takawwanat bihi-l-akwānu wa-stimdādātuhā
The holy manifestation of the Divine Attributes, through which the universes and their sustenance were formed

مَطْلَعِ شُمُوسِ الذَّاتِ فِي سَمَاءِ الأَسْمَاءِ وَالصِّفَاتْ

maṭlaʿi shumūsi-dh-dhāt fī samāʾi-l-asmāʾi wa-ṣ-ṣifāt
The emergence of the suns of the Divine Essence in the heaven of Divine Names and Attributes

وَمَنْبَعِ نُورِ الإِفَاضَاتِ فِي رِيَاضِ النِّسَبِ وَالإِضَافَاتْ

wa manbaʿi nūri-l-ifāḍāt fī riyāḍi-n-nisabi wa-l-iḍāfāt
The spring of the light of emanations in the gardens of relationships and associations

خَطِّ الوَحْدَةِ بَيْنَ قَوْسَيِّ الأَحَدِيَّةِ وَالوَاحِدِيَّة

khaṭṭi-l-waḥdati bayna qawsiyyi-l-aḥadiyati wa-l-wāḥidiyyah
The line of unity between the two arcs of Divine Singularity and Oneness

وَوَاسِطَةِ التَّنَزُّلِ مِنْ سَمَاءِ الأَزَلِيَّةِ إِلَى أَرْضِ الأَبَدِيَّة

wa wāsiṭati-t-tanazzuli min samāʾi-l-azaliyyah ilā arḍi-l-abadiyyah
And the means of descent, from the heaven of pre-eternity to the earth of eternity

النُّسْخَةِ الصُّغْرَى الَّتِي تَفَرَّعَتْ عَنْهَا الكُبْرَى

An-nuskhati-ṣ-ṣughrā al-latī tafarraʿat ʿanha-l-kubrā
The small version, from which branched the larger

وَالدُّرَّةِ البَيْضَاءِ الَّتِي تَنَزَّلَتْ إِلَى اليَاقُوتَةِ الحَمْرَاءْ

wa-d-durrati-l-bayḍāʾ al-latī tanazzalat ilā-l-yāqūtati-l-ḥamrāʾ
And the white pearl that descended to the red ruby

جَوْهَرِ الحَوَادِثِ الإِمْكَانِيَّةِ الَّتِي لَا تَخْلُو عَنِ الحَرَكَةِ وَالسُّكُونْ

jawhari-l-ḥawādithi-l-imkāniyyati-l-latī lā takhlū ʿan-il-ḥarakati wa-s-sukūn
The center of possible incidents, indivisible in movement and stillness

وَمَادَّةِ الكَلِمَةِ الفَهْوَانِيَّةِ الطَّالِعَةِ مِنْ كُنْهِ كُنْ إِلَى شَهَادَةِ فَيَكُونْ

wa māddati-l-kalimati-l-fahwāniyyati-ṭ-ṭāliʿati min kunhi Kun ilā shahādati fa-yakūn
And the matter of the uttered Divine Word, rising from the essence of ‘Be’ to the witnessed testimony of ‘It Becomes’

هَيُولَى الصُّوَرِ الَّتِي لَا تَتَجَلَّى بِإِحْدَاهَا مَرَّةً لِإِثْنَيْن

Hayūlā-ṣ-ṣuwari-l-latī lā tatajallā bi-iḥdāhā marratan li-ithnayn
The matter that does not manifest once to two persons

وَلَا بِصُورَةٍ مِنْهَا لِأَحَدٍ مَرَّتَيْن

wa lā bi-ṣūratin minhā li-aḥadin marratayn
Nor in a single image twice to one person

قُرْآنِ الجَمْعِ الشَّامِلِ لِلْمُمْتَنِعِ وَالعَدِيم

qurʾāni-l-jamʿi-sh-shāmili li-l-mumtaniʿi wa-l-ʿadīm
The *qurʾān* [gathering] of togetherness, encompassing the impossible and deprived

وَفُرْقَانِ الفَرْقِ الفَاصِلِ بَيْنَ الحَادِثِ وَالقَدِيم

wa furqāni-l-farqi-l-fāṣili bayna-l-ḥādithi wa-l-qadīm
And the *furqān* [dispersion] of definite separation between the incidental and eternal

صَائِمِ نَهَارِ "إِنِّي أَبِيتُ عِنْدَ رَبِّي"

ṣāʾimi nahāri "Innī abītu ʿinda rabbī"
He who fasts the morning of "I rest nightly with my Lord"

وَقَائِمِ لَيْلِ "تَنَامُ عَيْنَايَ وَلَا يَنَامُ قَلْبِي"

wa qāʾimi layli "Tanāmu ʿaynāya wa lā yanāmu qalbī"
And who prays the night of "My eyes sleep, but not my heart"

وَاسِطَةِ مَا بَيْنَ الوُجُودِ وَالعَدَمْ: "مَرَجَ البَحْرَيْنِ يَلْتَقِيَانْ"

wāsiṭati mā bayna-l-wujūdi wa-l-ʿadam: "Maraja-l-baḥrayni yaltaqiyān"
The medium between existence and non-existence: "He gathered the two seas whence they meet"

وَرَابِطَةِ تَعَلُّقِ الحُدُوثِ بِالقِدَمْ: "بَيْنَهُمَا بَرْزَخٌ لَا يَبْغِيَان"

wa rābiṭati taʿalluqi-l-ḥudūthi bi-l-qidam: "Baynahumā barzakhun lā yabghiyān"

And the connecting attachment between coming-to-be and eternity: "Between them is a barrier, they do not transgress"

فَذَلِكَ دَفْتَرِ الأَوَّلِ وَالآخِرْ

fa-dhālika daftari-l-awwali-wa-l-ākhir

That [he] is the tome of the First and Last

وَمَرْكَزِ إِحَاطَةِ البَاطِنِ وَالظَّاهِرْ

wa markazi iḥāṭati-l-bāṭini wa-ẓ-ẓāhir

And center of encompassing the Inward and Outward

حَبِيبِكَ الَّذِي اسْتَجْلَيْتَ بِهِ جَمَالَ ذَاتِكَ عَلَى مِنَصَّةِ تَجَلِّيَاتِكْ

ḥabībika al-ladhī istajlayta bihi jamāla Dhātika ʿalā minaṣṣati tajalliyātik

Your Beloved through whom You Manifested the Beauty of Your Essence upon the niche of Your Theophanies

وَنَصَبْتَهُ قِبْلَةً لِتَوَجُّهَاتِكَ فِي جَامِعِ جَمِيعِ تَجَلِّيَاتِكْ

wa naṣabtahu qiblatan li-tawajjuhātika fī jāmiʿi jamīʿi tajalliyātik

And whom you established as a direction for Your Gaze in the gathering of all Your Manifestations

وَخَلَعْتَ عَلَيْهِ خِلْعَةَ الصِّفَاتِ وَالأَسْمَاءْ

wa khalaʿta ʿalayhi khilʿata-ṣ-Ṣifāti wa-l-Asmāʾ

Clothing him in the dress of Divine Attributes and Names

وَتَوَّجْتَهُ بِتَاجِ الخِلَافَةِ العُظْمَى

wa tawwajtahu bi-tāji-l-khilāfati-l- ʿuẓmā
And adorning him with the crown of the Greatest Deputyship

وَأَسْرَيْتَ بِجَسَدِهِ يَقَظَةً مِنَ المَسْجِدِ الحَرَامِ إِلَى المَسْجِدِ الأَقْصَى

wa asrayta bi-jasadihi yaqaẓatan mina-l-masjidi-l-ḥarāmi ilā-l-masjidi-l-aqṣā
Taking him on a waking bodily journey from the Sanctified Mosque [Mecca] to the Furthest Mosque [Jerusalem]

حَتَّى انْتَهَى إِلَى سِدْرَةِ المُنْتَهَى وَتَرَقَّى إِلَى قَابِ قَوْسَيْنِ أَو أَدْنَى

ḥatta-ntahā ilā sidrati-l-muntahā wa taraqqā ilā qābi qawsayni aw adnā
Till he reached the Lote Tree, and ascended to Two Bows Length or Less

فَانْسَرَّ وَأَسَرَّ فُؤَادُهُ بِشُهُودِكَ حَيْثُ لَا صَبَاحَ وَلَا مَسَاء

Fa-nsarra wa asarra fuʾāduhu bi-shuhūdika ḥaythu lā ṣabāḥa wa lā masāʾ
Whence he became joyous, and his heart witnessed You. There, where there is neither morning nor night

"مَا كَذَبَ الفُؤَادُ مَا رَأَى"

"Mā kathaba-l-fuʾādu mā raʾā"
"Indeed, the heart does not lie in what it perceives"

وَأَقَرَّ بَصَرُهُ بِوُجُودِكَ حَيْثُ لَا خَلَاءَ وَلَا مَلَاء

wa aqarra baṣaruhu bi-wujūdika ḥaythu lā khalāʾa wa lā

malāʾ
His gaze affirming Your Being, where there is neither emptiness nor fullness

"مَا زَاغَ الْبَصَرُ وَمَا طَغَى"

"Mā zāgha-l-baṣaru wa mā ṭaghā"
"Indeed, the sight neither swerves nor transgresses"

صَلِّ اللهُمَّ عَلَيْهِ صَلَاةً يَصِلُ بِهَا فَرْعِي إِلَى أَصْلِي وَبَعْضِي إِلَى كُلِّي

ṣalli Allāhumma ʿalayhi ṣalātan yaṣilu bihā farʿī ilā aṣlī wa baʿḍī ilā kullī
Send prayers upon him, oh God, such that my branches reach my root, and parts to my entirety

لِتَتَّحِدَ ذَاتِي بِذَاتِهِ وَصِفَاتِي بِصِفَاتِه

li-tattaḥida dhātī bi-dhātihi wa ṣifātī bi-ṣifātih
So that my essence and attributes may unite with his

وَتَقَرَّ العَيْنُ بِالعَيْن وَيَفِرَّ البَيْنُ مِنَ البَيْن

wa taqarra-l-ʿaynu bi-l-ʿayn wa yafirra-l-baynu mina-l-bayn
Whence the eye (I) may find sweetness with the eye (I), and distance flees from the in-between

وَسَلِّمْ عَلَيْهِ سَلَاماً أَسْلَمُ بِهِ فِي مُتَابَعَتِهِ مِنَ التَّخَلُّفْ

wa sallim ʿalayhi salāman aslamu bihi fī mutābaʿatihi mina-t-takhalluf
And send salutations upon him, through which I may find safety in following him from tarrying

وَأَسْلَمُ فِي طَرِيقِ شَرِيعَتِهِ مِنَ التَّعَسُّفْ

wa aslamu fī ṭarīqi sharīʿatihi mina-t-taʿassuf
Finding safety in the way of his law from tyranny

لَأَفْتَحَ بَابَ مَحَبَّتِكَ إِيَّايَ بِمِفْتَاحِ مُتَابَعَتِهِ

li-aftaḥa bāba maḥabbatika iyyāya bi-miftāḥi mutābaʿatih
Opening the door of Your Love for me through the key of following him

وَأَشْهَدُكَ فِي حَوَاسِّي وَأَعْضَائِي مِنْ مِشْكَاةِ شَرْعِهِ وَطَاعَتِهِ

wa ash'haduka fī ḥawāssī wa aʿḍāʾī min mishkāti sharʿihi wa ṭāʿatih
Witnessing You in my senses and organs, through the niche of his way and obedience

وَأَدْخُلَ وَرَائَهُ إِلَى حِصْنِ "لَا إِلَهَ إِلَّا اللهُ"

wa adkhula warāʾahu ilā ḥiṣni "Lā ilāha illā-Allāh"
Entering behind him into the fortress of "There is no god but God"

وَفِي أَثَرِهِ إِلَى خَلْوَةِ "لِي وَقْتٌ مَعَ اللهِ"

wa fī atharihi ilā khalwati "Lī waqtun maʿa-Allāh"
And following his traces into the seclusion of "I have a time, only with my Lord"

إِذْ هُوَ بَابُكَ الَّذِي مَنْ لَمْ يَقْصُدْكَ مِنْهُ سُدَّتْ عَلَيْهِ الطُّرُقْ وَالأَبْوَابْ

idh huwa bābuka al-ladhī man lam yaqṣudka minhu suddat ʿalayhi-ṭ-ṭuruq wa-l-abwāb
For he is Your Gate, through other than whom whoever

intends You all their paths and doors are closed

وَرُدَّ بِعَصَا الأَدَبِ إِلَى اسْطَبْلِ الدَّوَابْ

wa rudda bi-ʿaṣa-l-adabi ilā isṭabli-d-dawāb
And they will be sent, with the staff of discipline, to the stable of animals

اللهُمَّ يَا رَبِّ يَا مَنْ لَيْسَ حِجَابُهُ إِلَّا النُّور

Allāhumma yā Rabbi yā ma-l-laysa ḥijābuhu illa-n-nūr
Oh God, my Lord, whose Veil is naught but Light

وَلَا خَفَائُهُ إِلَّا شِدَّةِ الظُّهُورْ

wa lā khafāʾuhu illā shiddati-ẓ-ẓuhūr
And His Hiddenness is naught but utter manifestation

أَسأَلُكَ بِكَ فِي مَرْتَبَةِ إِطْلَاقِكَ عَنْ كُلِّ تَقْيِيد

asʾaluka bika fī martabati iṭlāqika ʿan kulli taqyīd
I ask You, through You, in the station of Your Absolution from every limitation

الَّتِي تَفْعَلُ فِيهَا مَا تَشَاءُ وَتُرِيد

al-latī tafʿalu fīhā mā tashāʾu wa turīd
At which You do whatever You Will and Decree

وَبِكَشْفِكَ عَنْ ذَاتِكَ بِالعِلْمِ النُّورِيِّ

wa bi-kashfika ʿan dhātika bi-l-ʿilmi-n-nūriyy
Unveiling Your Essence through the luminous knowledge

وَتَحَوُّلِكَ فِي صُوَرِ أَسْمَائِكَ وَصِفَاتِكَ بِالوُجُودِ الصُّورِيِّ

wa taḥawwulika fī ṣuwarī Asmāʾika wa Ṣifātika bi-l-wujūdi-ṣ-ṣūriyyi
Turning in the Forms of Your Names and Attributes through the images of existence

أَنْ تُصَلِّيَ عَلَى سَيِّدِنَا مُحَمَّدٍ صَلَاةً

an tuṣalliya ʿalā sayyidinā Muḥammadin ṣalātan
That You send prayers
upon our master Muhammad ﷺ

تَكْحَلُ بِهَا أَبْصَارَنَا وَبَصَائِرَنَا بِالنُّورِ الْمَرْشُوشِ فِي الأَزَلْ

takḥalu bihā abṣāranā wa baṣāʾiranā bi-n-nūri-l-marshūshi fi-l-azal
Through which You may adorn our sights and insights with the [his] light dispersed in pre-eternity

حَتَّى نَشْهَدَ فَنَاءَ مَا لَمْ يَكُنْ وَبَقَاءَ مَا لَمْ يَزَلْ

ḥattā nashhada fanāʾa mā lam yakun wa baqāʾa mā lam yazal
So that we may witness the passing of what never was and subsistence of what always has been

وَنَرَى الأَشْيَاءَ كَمَا هِيَ فِي أَصْلِهَا مَعْدُومَةً مَفْقُودَةْ

wa nara-l-ashyāʾa kamā hiya fī aṣlihā maʿdūmatan mafqūdah
Seeing things as they are in origin: non-existent and lost

وَكَوْنَهَا لَمْ تَشُمَّ رَائِحَةَ الوُجُودِ فَضْلًا عَنْ كَونِهَا مَوْجُودَةْ

wa kawnahā lam tashummā rāʾiḥata-l-wujūdi faḍlan ʿan kawnihā mawjūdah
Never smelling the fragrance of being, much less existing

وَأَخْرِجْنَا اللهُمَّ بِالصَّلَاةِ عَلَيْهِ مِنْ ظُلْمَةِ أَنَانِيَّتِنَا إِلَى النُّورْ

wa akhrijnā Allāhumma bi-ṣ-ṣalāti ʿalayhi min ẓulmati anāniyyatinā ila-n-nūr

And take us, oh God, by sending benedictions upon him, from the darkness of our beings to the light

وَمِنْ قَبْرِ جِثْمَانِيَّتِنَا وَجِسْمَانِيَّتِنَا إِلَى جَمْعِ الحَشْرِ وَفَرْقِ النُّشُورْ

wa min qabri jithmāniyyatinā wa jismāniyyatinā ilā jamʿi-l-ḥashri wa farqi-n-nushūr

And from the tomb of our bodies to the gathering of resurrection and dispersion of spreading forth

وَأَفِضْ عَلَيْنَا مِنْ سَمَاءِ تَوْحِيدِكَ إِيَّاكَ مَا تُطَهِّرُنَا بِهِ مِنْ رِجْسِ الشِّرْكِ والإِشْرَاكْ

wa afiḍ ʿalaynā min samāʾi tawḥīdika iyyāka mā tuṭahhirunā bihi min rijsi-sh-shirki wa-l-ishrāk

And unfold upon us, from the Heaven of Your Own Unification, that which purifies us of the filth of polytheism and making partners with You

وأَنْعِشْنَا بِالمَوْتَةِ الأُولَى وَالوِلَادَةِ الثَّانِيَةْ

wa anʿishnā bi-l-mawtati-l-ūlā wa-l-wilādati-th-thāniyah

And revive us with the first death and second birth

وَأَحْيِنَا بِالحَيَاةِ البَاقِيَةِ فِي هَذِهِ الدُّنيَا الفَانِيَةْ

wa aḥyinā bi-l-ḥayāti-l-bāqiyati fī hādhihi-d-dunyā-l-fāniyah

And enliven us with an immortal life in this temporal world

واجْعَل لَنا نُورًا نَمْشِي بِهِ فِي النَّاسْ

wa-jʿal lanā nūran namshī bihi fi-n-nās
And grant us a light through which we may walk among the people

وَنَرَى بِهِ وَجْهَكَ أَيْنَمَا تَوَلَّيْنَا بِدُونِ اشْتِبَاهٍ وَلَا التِبَاسْ

wa narā bihi wajhaka aynamā tawallaynā bi-dūni-shtibāhin wa-la-l-tibās
Gazing through it upon Your Face wherever we turn, in neither confusion nor doubt

نَاظِرِينَ بِعَيْنَيْ الجَمْعِ وَالفَرْقْ

nāẓirīna bi-ʿaynayi-l-jamʿi wa-l-farq
Perceiving with the two eyes of gathering and separation

وَفَاصِلِينَ بِحُكْمِ الحَقِّ بَيْنَ البَاطِلِ وَالحَقْ

wa fāṣilīna bi-ḥukmi-l-Ḥaqqi bayna-l-bāṭili wa-l-ḥaqq
Separating with the judgment of the Real between falsehood and truth

دَالِّينَ بِكَ عَلَيْكْ وَهَادِينَ بِإِذْنِكَ إِلَيْكْ

dāllīna bika ʿalayk wa hādīna bi-idhnika ilayk
Pointing through You to You and guiding with Your Permission towards You

يَا أَرْحَمَ الرَّاحِمِينْ (ثلاث مرات)

yā arḥama-r-rāḥimīn x 3
Oh, Most Merciful of the merciful x 3

صَلِّ وَسَلِّمْ عَلَى سَيِّدِنَا مُحَمَّدٍ صَلَاةً تَتَقَبَّلُ بِهَا دُعَائَنَا

ṣalli wa sallim ʿalā sayyidinā Muḥammadin ṣalātan tataqabbalu bihā duʿāʾanā

Send Prayers and Salutations upon our master Muhammad, through which You may accept our supplication

وَتُحَقِّقُ بِهَا رَجَائَنَا

wa tuḥaqqiqu bihā rajāʾanā

And fulfill our hopes

وَعَلَى آلِهِ آلِ الشُّهودِ وَالعِرْفَانْ

wa ʿalā ālihi āli-sh-shuhūdi wa-l-ʿirfān

And upon his family, the people of witnessing and gnosis

وَأَصْحَابِهِ أَصْحَابِ الذَوْقِ وَالوِجْدَانْ

wa aṣḥābihi aṣḥābi-dh-dhawqi wa-l-wijdān

And his companions, those of spiritual taste and ecstasy

مَا انْتَشَرَتْ طُرَّةُ لَيْلِ الكَيَانْ وَأَسْفَرَتْ غُرَّةُ جَبِينِ العِيَانْ

ma-ntasharat ṭurratu layli-l-kayān wa asfarat ghurratu jabīni-l-ʿiyān

As the countenance of being's night spreads, and illumines the eyes of perception

آمين آمين آمين وَالحَمْدُ لله رَبِّ العَالَمِين

āmīn āmīn āmīn wa-l-ḥamdu lillāhi rabbi-l-ʿālamīn

Amen Amen Amen and All Praise is due to God the Lord of the Worlds.

www.ingramcontent.com/pod-product-compliance
Lightning Source LLC
Chambersburg PA
CBHW041130110526
44592CB00020B/2747
9781938058752